Chinese
in the Building
of the
U.S. West

GLOBE BOOK COMPANY
A Division of Simon & Schuster
Englewood Cliffs, New Jersey

Consultant:
Samuel C. Chu
Vice-chairman, Department of History
Ohio State University, Columbus, Ohio

Executive Editor: Stephen Lewin
Editorial Consultant: Phyllis Goldstein
Project Editor: Dan Zinkus
Art Director: Nancy Sharkey
Designer: Armando Baez
Production Manager: Winston Sukhnanand
Marketing Manager: Elmer Ildefonso
Book Design: Keithley & Associates
Maps and Diagrams: Function Thru Form Inc.
Electronic Page Production: Function Thru Form Inc.
Photo Research: Omni-Photo Communications, Inc.

Photo Acknowledgments
9: Library of Congress. 11: Bettmann Archive. 18: The Granger Collection. 21: Culver Pictures. 23: Bettmann Archive. 24: The Granger Collection. 27: Bettmann Archive. 35: Bettmann Archive. 39: The Granger Collection. 43: Denver Public Library. 47: California Historical Society Library. 48: Chinese Historical Society Library. 51: The Granger Collection. 52: Thorne Studio/C.L. DeVed. 55: The Bancroft Library. 59: Special College Division–University of Washington Libraries. 67: The Granger Collection. 69: The Granger Collection. 71: Bettmann Archive. 73: Bettmann Archive. 79: Idaho Historical Society. 83: California Historical Society Library. 86: San Francisco History Room, San Francisco Public Library.

Cover: New Year's Day in San Francisco's Chinatown, 1881 by Theodore Wores (1859-1939). Courtesy of Drs. Ben and A. Jess Shansan.

ISBN: 0-835-90488-1

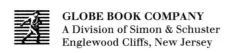

GLOBE BOOK COMPANY
A Division of Simon & Schuster
Englewood Cliffs, New Jersey

CONTENTS

THE HOMELAND

THINKING ABOUT THE CHAPTER

What factors encouraged large numbers of Chinese to leave their homes and settle in other countries, including the United States, in the 1800s?

A ccording to an old Chinese saying, "To be even one *li* [.3 miles, or .48 kilometers] from home is not as good as being home." Yet between 1840 and 1888, over 2 million people left China for other countries. Some journeyed across 7,000 miles [11,200 kilometers] of ocean to settle in the United States. Others made their way to Hawaii (then not a part of the United States), Canada, Australia, New Zealand, Southeast Asia, the West Indies, South America, and Africa.

SECTIONS

1 Dreams of *Hsiang*

2 Times of Trouble and Change

The decision to **emigrate**, or leave one's home country for another place, is never an easy one. For the Chinese, it was particularly difficult. The following poem, written in the 700s by Li Po, was popular with Chinese emigrants:

> So bright a gleam at the foot of my bed—
> Could there be a frost already?
> Lifting myself to look, I see that it is moon-
> light.
> Lowering my head, I dream of *hsiang*.

The word ***hsiang*** (sheeang) is one of the most emotion-filled words in the Chinese language. It means

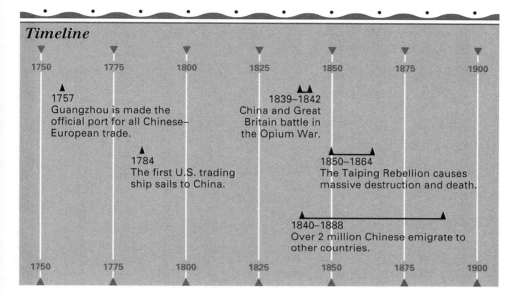

Timeline

1750   1775   1800   1825   1850   1875   1900

1757
Guangzhou is made the
official port for all Chinese–
European trade.

1839–1842
China and Great
Britain battle in
the Opium War.

1784
The first U.S. trading
ship sails to China.

1850–1864
The Taiping Rebellion causes
massive destruction and death.

1840–1888
Over 2 million Chinese emigrate to
other countries.

1750   1775   1800   1825   1850   1875   1900

"hometown" or "village." This chapter tells about the *hsiang* the emigrants recalled in their dreams. It also describes the events that led the emigrants to leave their homes and their families for what one folk song called a perilous journey across the seas.

1 DREAMS OF *HSIANG*

What was life like in China's villages and towns in the 19th century?

The *hsiang* the emigrants recalled in their dreams was in southeastern China. Nearly everyone who left China in the 19th century came from just two provinces, Guangdong (gwang-doong) and Fujian (foo-kyen). The two border each other and the South China Sea. They are separated from places farther north and west by mountains and hills.

The Two Provinces Southeastern China is a semitropical land, where temperatures rarely dip below freezing. Summers are warm and very wet, and winters mild but dry. In this region, rice is the most important crop. Most of the people in the two provinces were farmers. They grew rice, sugar cane, bananas, mangoes, peaches, and plums. Away

5

THE CHINESE HOMELAND

MANCHURIA

MONGOLIA

TIBET

40°N
SEA OF
JAPAN

Huang He (Yellow River)

Beijing

KOREA

JAPAN

C H I N A

Shanghai

30°N

Chang Jiang (Yangtze River)

EAST
CHINA
SEA

N
W E
S

INDIA

FUJIAN

25°N

BURMA
(MYANMAR)

(VIETNAM)

Guangzhou (Canton)   GUANGDONG
Taishan
Pearl River

FORMOSA
(TAIWAN)

PACIFIC
OCEAN

0   300 Miles

Hong Kong

SOUTH
CHINA SEA

0   300 Kilometers

(LAOS)

SIAM
(THAILAND)   ANNAM

115°E   120°E   125°E

In what part of China were the provinces of Guangdong and Fujian located? What bodies of water did they border?

from the river valleys, farmers carved great steps, called **terraces**, on the hillsides to add more land for crops.

Farmers throughout the region planted and harvested two and sometimes three crops a year. When it was too cold to plant rice, people raised ducks in their rice paddies. They also fished in the rivers and canals that crisscrossed the region. Other people turned to the sea for food. Yet no matter how hard the people of the two provinces worked and how little they wasted, there were still too many people on too little land.

The People Southeastern China had a more diverse population than other parts of the country. It included people of many different **regional groups**. People in these groups shared history, language, customs, and traditions.

Often, group differences divided the people of southeastern China. The city of Guangzhou (gwang-joh), or Canton, as it was called, was the capital of Guangdong, and its main port. People in Guangzhou and a district in the countryside nearby spoke a **dialect**, a form of a language spoken in a particular region, that other Chinese in Guangdong regarded as a foreign tongue. They could not understand what the people of Guangzhou were saying. Moreover, neither the inhabitants of Guangzhou nor the other Chinese in Guangdong could understand the Chinese spoken in North China. These groups could communicate only in writing.

The people of Guangzhou considered themselves superior to others in the region. They belonged to a group known as the Punti, the original settlers of the area. The newest group in the region were the Hakka, who began to move into the southeast during the 13th century. Members of a third group did not own any land in the region. They were the Tanka, the boat people of southeastern China. They lived on their boats and earned a living by running ferry services and by smuggling.

The Chinese Family Throughout China, the family was the most important group in everyone's life. Family members lived and worked together as a unit, sharing goals, values, and a common heritage. They believed that they owed a debt to their ancestors, who had made it possible for the family to survive to the present. They also felt that they had a duty to work together to ensure their family's future.

In an ideal Chinese family, several generations would live together in one large house or a series of smaller houses joined together. Such a household included grandparents, parents, their sons, the sons' wives and their children, and all unmarried daughters. Each member of a family had specific duties and responsibilities. The old were responsible for the care and teaching of the young. The young, in turn, had to honor and respect their elders.

Few families ever measured up to the ideal, since only the rich could afford to live in large family groups. Yet rich or poor, the people in a traditional Chinese family believed that their individual desires were less important than the needs of the family as a whole.

Village Life Most families lived in small villages clustered around a market town. People walked to town on special occasions. They went to trade, celebrate a holiday, hear a traveling storyteller, or see a theater troupe.

The village was the center of everyday life. There were no strangers in Chinese villages. People knew their neighbors and took an interest in everyone else's affairs. Villagers banded together for mutual protection and helped each other in times of trouble.

Often everyone in a village belonged to a single **clan**. A clan is a group of families that share a common ancestor. If several clans lived in a village or town, each had its own neighborhood. Members of a clan lent one another money, helped parents arrange marriages for their children, and settled family quarrels.

Most families had lived in the same village for generations. People were connected to their neighbors in hundreds of ways. They could count on their neighbors' support just as they could count on the support of other family members.

TAKING ANOTHER LOOK

1. What were the chief ways of making a living in the provinces of Guangdong and Fujian?
2. What was the center of everyday life for the people of southeastern China?
3. *CRITICAL THINKING* How do you think Chinese family values affected decisions about emigration?

2 TIMES OF TROUBLE AND CHANGE

Why did some Chinese leave their homes and families in the 19th century?

In the 1800s, China was home to about 400 million people, the vast majority of whom had little or no desire to live

This photograph shows a southern Chinese village during the 1800s. The village's main crop is rice, grown in the surrounding paddies.

anywhere else. But in the 1800s, large numbers of people—mostly from Guangdong and Fujian—left China to settle in the United States and other countries. Why?

Pressures to Emigrate The provinces of Guangdong and Fujian both had more people than they could feed. As early as 1500, the provinces had less farmland per person than most other parts of China. Many families there just barely survived even when their harvests were good. When wars, floods, or typhoons devastated their fields, many families did not have enough to eat.

In one county near Guangzhou, even in good years farmers produced only enough food for about a third of the people. When asked about their harvest, some villagers in Fujian would sadly reply that it was a "20 crop." In other years, they might brag about a "nothing crop." A "20 crop" was so small that 20 members of the clan would have to emigrate. A "nothing crop" was large enough that no one had to leave home.

It is not surprising then that many people in the region turned to the sea to earn a living. Their **junks**, the flat-bottomed Chinese sailing ships, could be found in every port along the coast of China. There the owners of the junks sold fish, rice, silk, and other goods. Gradually, over many years, they ventured farther and farther from home.

By the 15th century, traders from the two provinces were sailing to other parts of China and also to Africa, India, and countries throughout Southeast and East Asia. Little by little, some people from Guangdong and Fujian settled in other parts of Asia. When the Spanish conquered the Philippines in the 16th century, there were 20,000 Chinese living there. Thousands of Chinese merchants and artisans also lived in cities and towns in Thailand.

When Europeans arrived in Southeast Asia, the first Chinese they saw were from the two provinces. The two groups traded for many years in the ports of Southeast Asia before the first European ships arrived in Guangzhou and nearby Hong Kong. By the 1700s, European ships were no longer a novelty in South China.

European Invasions Europeans came to Asia to trade and to spread the Christian religion. By the 1700s, ships from Britain and France were pulling into ports in South China. Europeans and, later, people from the United States were eager to own Chinese silks, porcelain, jewels, and tea.

When Europeans and Americans reached China, however, they found that the Chinese were more than willing to sell to foreigners but had no interest in buying from them. The Chinese were satisfied with their own culture. To them, all foreigners were **barbarians**—people whose ways of living seemed crude and uncivilized.

The newcomers were angry at Chinese limits on trade. They wanted to sell as well as to buy, and they were determined to find something the Chinese would buy in large quantities. In the early 1800s, the British found such a product, the drug opium. It is as addictive as cocaine or heroin.

The British smuggled opium into China even though it was illegal to do so. The Chinese government tried desperately to halt the trade, but the British refused to stop. This conflict over opium led to a war between the two nations. The Opium War lasted from 1839 until 1842, when its more advanced weapons brought victory to Great Britain. Almost all of the fighting took place in Guangdong.

Wars and Rebellions During the years of fighting, Guangdong suffered greatly. Fields were destroyed and crops ruined. A few Chinese fled the country during the war. Others emigrated after it, when the emperor imposed heavy taxes to pay for the war. A poor region had become even poorer, and desperate clans now fought over land and water rights. Disinterested and often corrupt government officials made a bad situation worse. Then in 1850, the region exploded in what has been called the **Taiping Rebellion**.

The uprising was led by Hong Xiuchuan (sho-chu-an). He belonged to a Hakka clan from a village in the mountains west of Guangzhou. Hong told his followers that God had ordered him to overthrow the government and set up a new order based on equality. His message attracted people furious over hunger at home, corruption in government, and disrespectful foreigners in Guangzhou. Within a few years, millions had joined the uprising.

The rebellion lasted until 1864. During those years, Hong and his supporters conquered about half the country and nearly toppled the emperor. Over 600 cities were destroyed and some 20 million people killed. It was against this backdrop that thousands of Chinese left home.

The Decision to Leave Every emigrant had personal reasons for leaving home. One man who left as a boy came from a landless family in which the father worked as a night watchman for the village. The father was paid 12 baskets of rice a year when the harvest was good. When the harvest was poor, he was lucky to get half that amount. It was

Guangzhou was for many years the only port in China where Europeans were permitted to trade with the Chinese

EARLY SETTLERS

In 1781, a small band of settlers came to the green hills of the "Island of California." There, in the name of Charles II, king of Spain, they founded the village that is today the city of Los Angeles. Among those settlers was a man from China. The Spanish called him Antonio Rodriguez, but his real name is lost forever.

Rodriguez was not the only man from China in Hispanic America. There were hundreds of others. When the Spanish conquered the Philippines, many Chinese were already living there. They were skilled craftsworkers and traders, who aided the Spanish in many ways. They helped Spain organize its trade within East and Southeast Asia and even redesigned the Spanish ships so that they could carry more cargo safely across the oceans.

Chinese craftsworkers and merchants boarded those ships and sailed for the Americas, where they helped the Spanish build an empire. There were so many of them that the road from Acapulco to Mexico City was known as the China Road—*el Camino de la China*. Some emigrants stayed for just a few years and then returned to China. Others, like Rodriguez, remained in North America. They married Spanish or Native American women and gave up their dreams of returning home. In western Mexico and the southwestern part of the United States, Chino is still a common name.

then that the boy and his mother would search the harvested rice fields for any grains farmers might have dropped. Often the family had only salt and water to eat with their rice. For these people, and for many others like them, emigration was a last chance.

Until 1860, emigration was a crime punishable by death, yet that did not stop people from leaving. A few were men of means who saw an opportunity to strike it rich abroad. Some borrowed the money to pay for passage from their family or their clan. These emigrants headed for cities where other members of their clan already lived. Thousands thus made their way to Singapore, Malaya, Thailand, and the United States.

Most emigrants had little or no choice in where they ended up. They went wherever there was work and became **contract workers**. These emigrants agreed to work for a sponsor for five years in exchange for passage. Most contract workers were recruited by European companies with the help of Chinese agents. Others were taken prisoner in violent clan fights or during the Taiping Rebellion and then sold to recruiters.

Those Left Behind Almost all of the emigrants were young married men. Single women from respectable Chinese families did not travel far from home, and married women were even less likely to leave home. They were tied by custom and tradition to their homes and villages.

Custom was not the only reason women and young children stayed at home. Many families could barely scrape together enough money for one fare. They could not afford any additional passage money. Also, everyone thought that the separation was temporary. The men would be gone for just a few years—just long enough to make their fortune.

Although most emigrants were never able to save enough money to return, few forgot their families. Most sent money home regularly. Taishan, for example, had long been one of the poorest districts in Guangdong. By the early 1900s, it had become one of the most prosperous districts in China, with electric lights, modern buildings, paved roads, and even a railroad. No other district had better schools or a larger percentage of children in school. The money came from Chinese who had gone to the United States to work and who sent money back to their families.

TAKING ANOTHER LOOK

1. Why did people from Guangdong and Fujian first begin to emigrate from those provinces in the 15th century?
2. How did the arrival of Europeans and Americans affect Chinese emigration?
3. *CRITICAL THINKING* How do you think Chinese attitudes toward emigration might have been different if whole families could have afforded to leave China?

KEY IDEAS

1 Dreams of *Hsiang*

- Nearly everyone who left China in the 19th century came from one of just two provinces, Guangdong and Fujian, in the southeastern part of China.
- The people of southeastern China relied not only on the land but also on the sea to earn their livings.
- Southeastern China had a diverse population that included three major groups—the Punti, the Hakka, and the Tanka.
- The family was the most important group in China, and family members lived and worked together.
- Most people in China lived in small villages clustered around a market town. Often everyone in a village belonged to a single clan.

2 Times of Trouble and Change

- People from Guangdong and Fujian traded and settled in other parts of the world from the 15th century on.
- Europeans began arriving in Asia in significant numbers in the 16th century. They came to trade and to spread Christianity.
- The Chinese lost the war they fought with the British over the opium trade in the years from 1839 to 1842.
- The Taiping Rebellion caused turmoil in China from 1850 until 1864.
- Between 1840 and 1888, over 2 million Chinese emigrated to other parts of the world.

WHO, WHAT, WHERE

1. **Where** in China are Guangdong and Fujian located?
2. **What** is a regional group?
3. **What** is an emigrant?
4. **What** groups of people began to arrive in China in the 17th and 18th centuries?
5. **What** countries were involved in the Opium War?
6. **Where** was the Opium War for the most part fought?
7. **What** was the Taiping Rebellion?

8. **Who** were the contract workers?

9. **Where** did emigrants from China settle?

UNDERSTANDING THE CHAPTER

1. In what ways did the family unit shape life in southeastern China?

2. What was life like in the villages of southeastern China?

3. How did the arrival of Europeans and Americans change life in southeastern China?

4. What events encouraged emigration from China?

MAKING CONNECTIONS

1. What was the connection between the geography of southeastern China and the growth of emigration?

2. What was the connection between the Opium War and the growth of emigration?

3. What was the connection between traditional family values and the fact that relatively few women emigrated from China?

WRITING ABOUT HISTORY

1. Reread the poem by Li Po on page 4. Then imagine that you are a farmer from the province of Fujian who has been forced to emigrate from China. Write a poem in the same style as Li Po's in which you express your feelings about emigration.

2. Write an advertisement for overseas jobs that you think would have attracted young Chinese contract workers in the 1800s.

3. Imagine that you are a resident of a small village in Guangdong province near Guangzhou. The year is 1851. A member of your clan has already emigrated to Thailand and has written urging you to follow. Write a letter in response, reviewing the events that have taken place in the province in the past several years and giving your decision about emigrating.

2

THE CALL OF THE GOLD MOUNTAIN

THINKING ABOUT THE CHAPTER

How did the California gold rush affect early Chinese immigration to the United States?

I n the summer of 1848, even the tiniest villages in Guangdong buzzed with news of a gold strike in California, over 7,000 miles [11,200 kilometers] away. The villagers learned about the discovery in letters from Chinese merchants in San Francisco. Some say that Chum Ming, a merchant who sold tea, shawls, and other goods in the city before he took to the hills in search of gold, sent the first letter.

Some villagers doubted the story at first. They did not become believers until 1850, when the first adventurers returned to China with gold in their pockets. Many years later, Pyau Ling, a Chinese American historian, said of the reaction in China to the news, "The call of the Gold Mountain, the name given by the Chinese laborers to California, was ringing in the air." Thousands answered that call. In 1850 alone, 45 ships left Hong Kong for San Francisco. Each had nearly 500 passengers packed in its cargo hold. In California, those passengers would join thousands of other adventurers from every state in the United States and from almost every continent in the world.

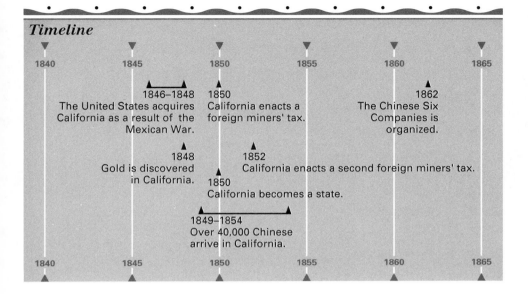

Timeline

1846–1848 The United States acquires California as a result of the Mexican War.

1850 California enacts a foreign miners' tax.

1862 The Chinese Six Companies is organized.

1848 Gold is discovered in California.

1852 California enacts a second foreign miners' tax.

1850 California becomes a state.

1849–1854 Over 40,000 Chinese arrive in California.

1. THE JOURNEY EAST

Who in China responded to the news of a gold rush and how did they get to California?

The first Chinese to arrive in San Francisco after the discovery of gold were not miners. They were professionals with little interest in digging for gold. They saw in California another way to get rich. They would supply the miners with food, tools, clothing, and other supplies. Some were merchants, while others were **artisans**, or craftsworkers.

An Ocean Away In 1848, California was in many ways closer to China than it was to other parts of the United States. People in those days measured distance not only in miles but also in time and ease of travel. New York was only 3,000 miles [4,800 kilometers] from San Francisco, but the trip overland took many months. A trip by ship around South America could be almost as long and just as hazardous.

Californians could have gotten supplies in Mexico. It was California's closest neighbor. However, the United States and Mexico had just fought the Mexican War (1846–48) and feelings still ran high. So Californians increasingly looked across the Pacific Ocean to China for needed goods.

San Francisco before the gold rush was a quiet little California town, as this view of the port drawn in 1849 illustrates.

Chinese merchants were quick to take advantage of the opportunity. They supplied food, tools, clothing, and other essentials to gold seekers. A U.S. minister reported, "Soon as the news of the discovery of gold reached [Chinese] ports, ships were loaded and dispatched to the California market." One miner reported, "Were it not for the Chinese, we might have starved the first year."

Workers in Demand The Chinese provided the miners with more than just food and other goods. Artisans as well as merchants accompanied the shiploads of supplies. When the news of the gold rush had reached San Francisco, many merchants had put up signs that said, "Gone to the Diggings. Help yourself. Put your money in the cash drawer." Others, like Chum Ming, did not bother to post a sign. They just left. So did thousands of workers.

Yet there was work that had to be done. Even adventurers need food, clothing, shelter, and tools. Hundreds of Chinese responded to the opportunities promised in advertisements distributed by foreign shipping companies. These ads claimed that in California the Chinese would find jobs at high wages in a land pictured as paradise. Among those lured by the ads were doctors, engineers, ironsmiths, and carpenters. Once they arrived in California, they immediately went to work outfitting the gold seekers. Chinese carpenters, for example, built hundreds of houses that could be quickly assembled. Those houses allowed whole towns to spring up almost overnight.

Welcome Strangers Despite their fears about living among "red haired, green eyed foreign devils with hairy faces," the early arrivals felt welcome. Lai Chun-Chuen, a San Francisco merchant, noted that he and other Chinese were "greeted with favor" by the Americans. He said of the relationship between the two peoples, "Each treated the other with politeness. From far and near we came and were pleased."

Newly arrived Chinese were invited to celebrations of California's admission to the Union in 1850. At many of the celebrations, the Chinese were urged to tell their "friends in China that in coming to this country, they will find welcome and protection." The Chinese took the speakers at their word. They encouraged their relatives to seek their fortunes in the "Land of the Gold Mountain."

Within a few years, thousands of Chinese were pouring into California. Between 1849 and 1854, over 40,000 Chinese arrived in San Francisco. For the most part, these were not well-to-do merchants or artisans. They were the sons of poor peasant farmers and fishers from Guangdong and Fujian. Almost all were young—the average age was about 25—and they felt they had little to lose by coming to a strange land.

Some were experienced miners who had worked in the goldfields of Borneo, in Southeast Asia. But most were simply young adventurers with nothing to lose and everything to gain. All they needed was the money to buy a ticket to the Land of the Gold Mountain.

A Matter of Money In the mid–1800s, a ticket to the United States from China cost about $40, sometimes a little more. At the height of the gold rush, the price went up to $200, as shipping companies took advantage of the boom. That price was a huge sum of money at the time. In the United States in the 1850s, many workers earned just $1 a week. In China, people earned even less.

The early arrivals from China—merchants and artisans—could afford a ticket, but those who arrived later rarely had enough money to come without help. Chinese merchants in San Francisco explained how these young men were able to come to California:

Some have borrowed the small amount necessary, to be returned with unusual interest, on account of the risk; some have been furnished with money without interest by their friends and relations, and some again, but much the smaller portion, have received advances in money, to be returned out of the profits of the adventure. The usual apportionment of the profits is about three tenths to the lender of the money.

The price of a ticket was only part of the money required to emigrate. The men also needed money to live on in Hong Kong and other ports while they waited for the next ship to the United States. Once the men reached California, they needed money to buy supplies before they left for the goldfields.

Sailing to the Gold Mountain The length of the journey depended on the ship and the winds. The most fortunate travelers went on clippers, then the fastest sailing ships in the world. The journey from Hong Kong to San Francisco by clipper took just a little over four weeks if the winds cooperated. It was not an easy journey even for first-class passengers, and the Chinese did not travel first class. Most traveled **steerage**. That meant that they were housed in the airless cargo hold of the ship and jammed into narrow bunks several rows deep. Huie Kin, a Chinese immigrant, recalled his voyage to San Francisco:

> Finally, the day was set for the ship to sail. We were two full months or more on our way. . . . When the wind was good and strong, we made much headway. But for days there would be no wind, the sails and ropes would hang lifeless from the masts, and the ship would drift idly on the smooth sea, while the sailors amused themselves by fishing. Occasionally, head winds became so strong as to force us back.

The day the emigrants saw California for the first time was one that they never forgot. Huie Kin wrote, "The feeling that welled up in us was indescribable." Another immigrant told of "gazing in silent wonder at the new land."

Chinese immigrants arriving in San Francisco often carried packages of bedding, clothing, and personal effects slung from bamboo poles.

When the gangway finally came down, the travelers rolled up their bedding, packed their baskets, and filed off the ship in long lines.

In those days, people could enter the United States freely. There were no immigration laws as yet, so people came and went with few questions asked. Still, the newcomers needed help, and such help came from earlier arrivals. As Huie Kin recalled:

> Out of the general babble, someone called out in our local dialect, and, like sheep recognizing the voice only, we blindly followed, and soon were piling into one of the waiting wagons. Everything was so strange and so exciting that my memory of the landing is just a big blur.

TAKING ANOTHER LOOK

1. What opportunities did the California gold rush provide Chinese immigrants?
2. How did poor Chinese immigrants pay for their journey to California?
3. *CRITICAL THINKING* Why do you think Americans at California's celebrations of statehood encouraged the Chinese to immigrate?

2 IN THE GOLDFIELDS
What was life like for the Chinese in the goldfields?

San Francisco was the starting point for Chinese gold seekers. As soon as they landed, they bought supplies and made their way to the goldfields (see map, page 36). Most traveled on foot, carrying their supplies on bamboo poles. Earlier arrivals had already swept through the area, skimming the gold that was easiest to find. The newcomers were not concerned. After all, some of them were experienced miners, eager to use their skills in California.

Life in the Mining Camps The Chinese came to the goldfields in groups of 10 or even 20. When they arrived, they, like the other adventurers, settled in a nearby mining camp. The camps were as rough as the men who lived and worked in them. Boardinghouses, restaurants, saloons, gambling houses, and stores stood side by side along the main, and often only, street in town. The Chinese put up their cabins a little apart from the others. There they formed a small community within the larger one.

Unlike most other miners, the Chinese had come to California with other men from their village or clan. Not only did they work together, but they also helped one another in times of trouble. Although the Chinese tended to keep to themselves, they were not unfriendly. They were willing to share their knowledge and skills with others in the fields, and many offered food and medicine to those in need. One miner, Ah Sang, became a legend in the goldfields.

In China, some say, Ah Sang had been a scholar who studied medicine. In California, other Chinese would come to him whenever they were ill or hurt. Before long, his skill attracted other miners as well. His remedies were so successful that the miners persuaded him to give up his search for gold and start a clinic.

Not surprisingly, many miners suffered from back trouble, chills, fevers, rheumatism, malaria, and dysentery. Scurvy was common because the miners ate no fresh fruit or vegetables. They lived mainly on salted and pickled meat. Only the Chinese bothered to wash. The others did not want to take the time. As a result, they had a running battle with fleas, lice, and other disease-carrying pests. Ah Sang's practice soon outgrew the hotel he used as his first clinic. In time, he built a hospital with 50 beds, which became one of the leading hospitals in the state.

Searching for Gold In 1849, miners had **panned** for gold in rivers and streams. They would dig up a mixture of dirt and sand from a riverbed, dump the mixture into baskets, tin cups, old hats, or even blankets, and add a little water. The gold, which is heavier than dirt, would settle to the bottom, while the dirt floated on the water.

Before long, people used a faster and more efficient method, the **cradle**. This was a rectangular, wooden box mounted on rockers that looked much like a baby's cradle. It was open at one end, however, and had a hopper at the other end. The miner would shovel dirt from the riverbed into the hopper, pour in water, and then rock the cradle fiercely until the sand washed through the coarse sieve at the bottom of the hopper. The

This early engraving of Chinese at work in the gold fields of California shows one of the miners using a cradle to separate gold ore from the dirt and sand.

heavier gold was caught by cleats nailed to the bottom of the box.

Both the pan and the cradle required patience and endurance. Many adventurers from Europe and the United States had neither. If they did not find gold quickly,

Mining camps grew into small towns almost overnight. This 1852 view shows Columbia, California, in the foothills of the Sierra Nevada mountains

they simply moved on. As latecomers to the goldfields, the Chinese took advantage of the opportunity. Merchants formed companies that bought up abandoned claims. They then hired newcomers to work those claims. A team of men would work together to retrieve gold from a river bottom. Some built water wheels to wash the dirt. Others put up dams to divert water from the river bottom. Then miners could easily remove whatever gold was there.

Such methods required cooperation and teamwork, but the results were often impressive. For example, four Chinese miners near Round Trent, California, bought an abandoned claim for a few hundred dollars. In two days time, they uncovered $4,000 worth of gold. Before they had a chance to enjoy their success, however, a "rush of white men" overran their claim.

Trouble in the Goldfields Many U.S. miners resented foreign miners. In some camps, they banded together to drive the foreigners out. When the foreigners stood up for their rights, there were fierce fights.

In 1850, at the request of gold seekers from the United States, California passed a foreign miners' tax. Every miner who was not a U.S. citizen had to pay a fee of $20 a month. In 1851, the law was repealed, but another tax, with a rate of $3 a month, was passed the following year.

The 1852 tax was aimed at Chinese miners, but it was collected from all Chinese whether or not they mined for a living. By that time, the Chinese were the largest group of foreigners in the goldfields. They made up about 10 percent of California's population. As their numbers grew, hostility toward them increased.

In a number of camps, groups of U.S. miners burned cabins and mining equipment owned by the Chinese. In other places, the Chinese were beaten or shot. Notices went up around some mining camps warning the Chinese to stay away. Although some returned to China, many headed for other goldfields or took jobs in hard-rock mines.

Hard-Rock Mining By the early 1850s, gold mining was changing. Miners could no longer find much gold in the rivers and streams of California. Now they had to dig for gold by sinking shafts deep in the earth and blasting tunnels through hard rock. Hard-rock mining required expensive tools and other equipment, and most gold seekers did not have the money to buy such tools. The new mine owners were investors, who bought expensive equipment and then hired laborers. Often those laborers were Chinese, who were willing to work for less money than U.S. miners.

At first, no one cared. But as the chances of striking it rich lessened, many gold seekers were eager to find other jobs in California. They deeply resented losing out to foreigners. A San Francisco newspaper that had earlier welcomed the Chinese now claimed that their training in the goldfields of Borneo gave them an "unfair advantage" over the less experienced U.S. miners. Many U.S. miners agreed. They persuaded the owners of the hard-rock mines not to hire foreigners. They also persuaded the state to pass laws barring the Chinese from becoming U.S. citizens.

More Chinese now headed for the goldfields of Colorado, Nevada, Idaho, and other parts of the U.S. West. Others continued to scratch for gold in the rivers and streams. They focused on the "$2-a-day" claims no one else wanted. Others headed for San Francisco where they found jobs and a way of life that reminded many of home.

1. Name two ways the Chinese differed from other gold seekers.

2. Name two ways the Chinese were like other gold seekers.

3. *CRITICAL THINKING* Why do you think tolerance disappeared as times got tough in the mining camps? What does your answer suggest about factors that contribute to the growth of prejudice?

3 BUILDING A COMMUNITY

How did the Chinese keep their culture alive in the United States?

As more and more Chinese came to California, a Chinese town grew up within San Francisco's city limits. Known as Chinatown, by the 1850s it covered 15 city blocks and contained dozens of stores, pharmacies, restaurants, herb shops, boardinghouses, butcher shops, and tailors. Within those blocks, the newcomers struggled to learn American ways so they could adapt to life in the United States. Yet they also tried to preserve their old way of life.

A Home Away From Home To outsiders, Chinatown was a mysterious place. In the mid–1850s, a San Francisco newspaper described the community this way.

> The majority of houses were of Chinese importation and were stores, stocked with hams, tea, dried fish, dried ducks, and other . . . Chinese eatables, besides copper pots and kettles, fans, shawls, chessmen, and all sorts of curiosities. Suspended over the doors were brilliantly-colored boards . . . covered with Chinese characters . . . while the streets were thronged.

To the Chinese, Chinatown was a home away from home. It was a place where workers could relax in the evenings after long hours in factories, in stores, or on the wharf. On the weekends, they were joined by men from the mining camps. There they, too, found familiar food, people who spoke their language, and traditional pastimes and occasions for celebrations.

Chinatown in those days was a bachelor community, where many residents slept in shifts in boardinghouses, attics, and cellars. There were only a handful of Chinese women in California. Chinatown was also a community of **sojourners**. A sojourner is someone who comes for a visit and then returns home. Almost everyone in Chinatown planned to return to China as soon as he made his fortune. But few got rich. Most only managed a few trips home to see wives and children before returning to California.

Associations From the start, the immigrants formed family and clan associations. The family associations, or *fongs*, ran club houses that were both residences and social centers. Each clan would start a temple. When a man died, the clan saw to it that his bones or ashes were shipped back to China for proper burial. Some also provided police and garbage service.

Many of these associations were led by well-to-do Chinese

By the late 1800s, San Francisco's Chinatown was a bustling place, where immigrants could find familiar foods and products sold by merchants who spoke their language.

EATING CHINESE FOOD— AMERICAN STYLE

When people in the United States think of Chinese food, chop suey is often the first food to come to mind. Yet no one in China eats chop suey. It is a U.S. dish. No one knows for sure who invented it. According to one legend, it was created in the 1860s when a group of hungry U.S. miners went looking for something to eat after a night out in San Francisco. The only place still open was a tiny Chinese restaurant that had never served U.S. miners before. The cook was ready to close but could not speak English well enough to communicate that to the hungry men. So he threw together all of his leftovers and served it to them. They loved it and asked what it was called. He told them it was *chop suey*. In Cantonese, *chop suey* is a finely chopped dish or a hash. The rest is history. The people of the United States have been eating *chop suey* ever since. They also enjoy dozens of more authentic Chinese dishes.

merchants. They handed out jobs, settled disputes, and acted as spokesmen for relatives in their dealings with other groups. Many merchants kept a place above their stores for relatives to stay when they first arrived in California from China. Often a clan would begin to specialize in a particular trade, product, or business. One clan might own a number of fruit stores. Another might specialize in restaurants or tailoring shops.

The Chinese also formed district associations. Members all came from the same county or district in China. Known as the **huiguan** (hwee-gwan), these associations, too, helped newcomers. They also saw to it that the newcomers paid off their debts before they returned to China. In San Francisco, several of these district associations joined together in the early 1850s to form the **Chinese Six Companies**. Later, the group expanded to include more than six associations. The Six Companies acted as a government within Chinatown. It defended the Chinese from outside threats, especially prejudice and discrimination, by fighting unjust laws and practices. As early as 1852, Norman Asing, a leader of the Six Companies was sending letters of protest to the governor of California. In one, he wrote:

> The effect of your late message has been thus far to prejudice the public mind against my people, to enable those who wait the opportunity to hunt them down, and rob them of their toil. . . . We would beg to remind you that when your nation was a wilderness, and the nation from which you spring barbarous [uncivilized], we exercised most of the arts and virtues of civilized life.

The Six Companies also tried to keep order within Chinatown. Those efforts brought the group into conflict with secret societies known as **tongs**. *Tongs* were patterned after similar groups in Guangdong. Asked why he joined, a member explained, "We are strangers in a strange country. We must have an organization to control our country fellows and develop our friendship."

Some *tongs* went beyond mutual assistance. They became involved in gambling and other illegal practices. From time to time, those activities led to conflicts with the Six Companies.

By the 1860s, Chinatown was changing. It was less a stopping place for sojourners and more a permanent home. Some men were now going back to China, not to live or to visit, but to bring back their wives and children. The Chinese were gradually becoming Chinese Americans.

TAKING ANOTHER LOOK

1. How did storekeepers help the newcomers feel at home in a strange land?
2. What groups helped the newcomers adjust to life in the United States?
3. *CRITICAL THINKING* Reread Norman Asing's letter to the governor above. What does it suggest about the way others viewed the Chinese? About the way the Chinese saw themselves?

KEY IDEAS

1 The Journey East

- The first Chinese to arrive in San Francisco after the discovery of gold were merchants and artisans who provided goods and services for miners and other adventurers.
- The Chinese who headed for the goldfields later came mainly from poor families in Guangdong and Fujian.
- Many young Chinese borrowed money to come to California.

2 In the Goldfields

- Some of the Chinese were experienced miners. Through teamwork, the Chinese found gold in claims that other miners had abandoned.
- Chinese customs and traditions eased the newcomers' adjustment to life in the mining camps.
- When hard-rock mines opened, many Chinese found jobs in them.
- The Chinese were often forced out of the mines and the goldfields by U.S. miners.

3 Building a Community

- In the United States, Chinese immigrants built up new communities in many places.
- Traditional Chinese institutions made life easier for the newcomers to San Francisco.

WHO, WHAT, WHERE

1. **Where** did most of the Chinese gold miners in California come from?
2. **What** opportunities attracted the first arrivals?
3. **Where** were the goldfields?
4. **What** was the foreign miners' tax of 1852?
5. **What** was a family association?
6. **What** did clan associations do for their members?
7. **What** was the Chinese Six Companies?
8. **What** was a *tong*?

1. How did most Chinese get the money they needed to come to California?

2. Why did Chinese miners work claims that other miners had abandoned?

3. How did the growth of hard-rock mining change life in the goldfields?

4. How did traditional Chinese institutions help the newcomers adjust to life in the United States?

MAKING CONNECTIONS

1. How was a war between the United States and Mexico connected with the growing trade between California and China?

2. What was the connection between California laws aimed at Chinese immigrants and the arrival of Chinese immigrants in other states?

3. What was the connection between the growing discrimination against the Chinese and the kinds of associations the Chinese formed in San Francisco?

WRITING ABOUT HISTORY

1. Imagine that you are a Chinese immigrant who has just arrived in San Francisco. Write a letter to your family back in Fujian describing your voyage.

2. After the Manchu conquered China in the 17th century, they forced all Chinese men to wear queues, or braids, as a sign that they were a conquered people. In China, the men hated their queues and were eager to cut them off. But in the United States, the queues became a badge of honor, and an attack on a braid was considered an insult. Write a brief paragraph explaining why you think the Chinese in the United States defended the wearing of braids.

3. Imagine that you are a Chinese gold miner in California. Write a letter to that state's governor giving your reaction to the 1852 foreign miners' tax.

CHAPTER 3

A WORK OF GIANTS

THINKING ABOUT THE CHAPTER

What part did Chinese workers play in the building of the first transcontinental railroad?

SECTIONS

1 Linking East and West

2 Building the Great Iron Trail

Just after the Civil War, one of the most dramatic chapters in the building of the U.S. West began. It was a chapter in which Chinese played a leading role. They helped build the railroad that linked the eastern states with California and the territories west of the Mississippi. Civil War hero General William T. Sherman said that the construction of such a transcontinental railroad would be "a work of giants." Workers would have to lay track through snow-capped mountains, across deep canyons, and over miles of desert.

The Chinese did almost all of the work on the rail line from California, while Irish immigrants built the railroad from the east. Even though it was dangerous work that few people wanted, the Chinese had to overcome prejudice and discrimination to get it.

Little is known about the individual men who worked on the railroad. No one interviewed them, and they themselves did not write many letters or keep diaries. The little we do know comes from observers who watched in amazement as the Chinese built a railroad through some of the most rugged land in North America.

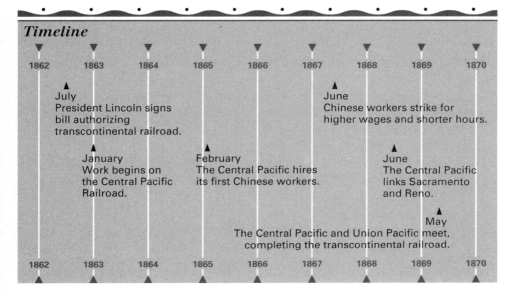

| 1862 | 1863 | 1864 | 1865 | 1866 | 1867 | 1868 | 1869 | 1870 |

July
President Lincoln signs bill authorizing transcontinental railroad.

June
Chinese workers strike for higher wages and shorter hours.

January
Work begins on the Central Pacific Railroad.

February
The Central Pacific hires its first Chinese workers.

June
The Central Pacific links Sacramento and Reno.

May
The Central Pacific and Union Pacific meet, completing the transcontinental railroad.

| 1862 | 1863 | 1864 | 1865 | 1866 | 1867 | 1868 | 1869 | 1870 |

1 LINKING EAST AND WEST

Why was building a transcontinental railroad an important goal for the United States in the 1860s?

On July 1, 1862, President Abraham Lincoln signed into law a bill that called for the greatest engineering feat the nation had ever attempted. Known as the Pacific Railroad Act, it authorized the building of a railroad to link the nation's Atlantic and Pacific coasts.

A Matter of National Importance The need for a transcontinental railroad was obvious to most Americans in the 1860s. Gold and silver from western mines were needed to help pay for the Civil War. Yet in those days, there were no railroads west of Omaha, in the territory of Nebraska, so miners had to send their ore east by wagon train. It was faster to go by water, but the voyage around South America turned a 3,000-mile [4,800-kilometer] trip into a perilous 17,000-mile [27,200-kilometer] one. Many ships sank in the treacherous waters around Cape Horn, the southernmost part of South America. A shortcut across the **Isthmus of Panama**, the narrow strip of land where North and South America meet, often proved as dangerous as the other routes.

No one wanted a transcontinental railroad more than the people of California, since without it, their state would not grow. California business leaders had started pushing for a transcontinental railroad soon after the gold rush began in 1849. Now their dream was about to come true.

The law that Lincoln signed gave two companies permission to build a transcontinental railroad. The Union Pacific, based in the eastern United States, had the right to build west from Omaha to the eastern border of California. A California company called the Central Pacific would build east from Sacramento, the state capital. When the two railroads met, the transcontinental railroad would be complete.

In many ways, the Union Pacific had the easier job. The land west of Omaha rises gradually, while the land east of Sacramento climbs from nearly sea level to over 7,000 feet [2,100 meters] above sea level within just 100 miles [160 kilometers]. Some people claimed that it was impossible to build a railroad across such terrain. In the 1860s, almost all of the work had to be done by hand.

Organizing the Central Pacific Still, the owners of the Central Pacific were determined to succeed. They included merchants Collis P. Huntington and Mark Hopkins, grocer Leland Stanford, gold miner Charles Crocker, and engineer Theodore Judah. When Lincoln signed the railroad bill, the partners began assembling supplies for the actual building.

By the end of 1862, the Central Pacific had enough equipment in California to start work. On January 8, 1863, the company held groundbreaking ceremonies in Sacramento. Newspapers reported that a large crowd cheered as Stanford, by then the governor of California, turned over the first shovelful of dirt. One reporter wrote:

> Everyone felt happy because after so many years
> of dreaming, scheming, talking, and toiling, they
> saw with their own eyes the actual commence-
> ment of a Pacific railroad.

In Search of Workers The days that followed were not as bright. Crocker was in charge of the construction, and he faced a huge task. There were not many people in California in 1863 and even though most of them wanted a railroad, few

had any interest in building one. Workers were hard to find and even harder to keep. Nine out of ten stayed on the job just one week.

Although he searched frantically for help, Crocker refused to hire Chinese workers. Crocker thought that they were too small and too weak to blast and pickax their way through the mountains. Some say the man who changed Crocker's mind was Ah Sing, who worked for him as a servant. Ah Sing is said to have reminded Crocker that it was the Chinese who built the Great Wall of China, one of the greatest engineering feats of all time. In February 1865, the desperate Crocker hired 50 Chinese workers on a trial basis.

James Strobridge, the construction boss, did not like the idea nor did the other workers. Strobridge tried to reassure his men by telling them that the Chinese were bound to fail his test. The men were certain he was right when the Chinese marched into camp in blue cotton pajama-like clothing with their faces shadowed by large, wide-brimmed straw hats.

Strobridge showed the Chinese what to do, and they immediately went to work. They moved as a team, with one man supervising as the others carried out a variety of tasks. As one group shoveled, another group would cart the dirt away. Two or three times a day, a man would serve hot tea.

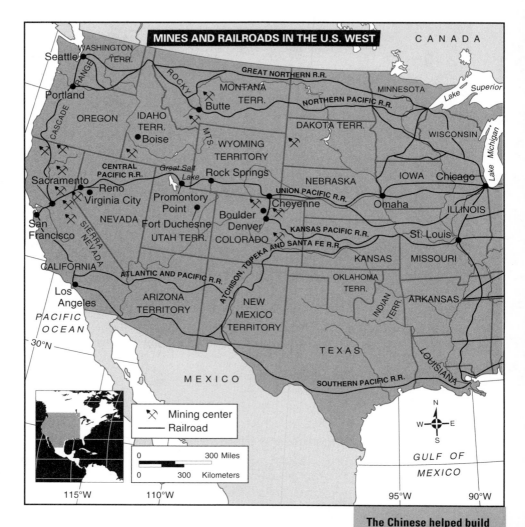

MINES AND RAILROADS IN THE U.S. WEST

CANADA

Seattle
WASHINGTON TERR.
Portland
OREGON
IDAHO TERR.
Boise
MONTANA TERR.
Butte
ROCKY MTS
GREAT NORTHERN R.R.
NORTHERN PACIFIC R.R.
MINNESOTA
Lake Superior
DAKOTA TERR.
WISCONSIN
Lake Michigan
CENTRAL PACIFIC R.R.
Great Salt Lake
Rock Springs
WYOMING TERRITORY
Sacramento
Reno
Virginia City
Promontory Point
NEVADA
Fort Duchesne
UTAH TERR.
Boulder
Denver
COLORADO
NEBRASKA
UNION PACIFIC R.R.
Cheyenne
Omaha
IOWA
Chicago
ILLINOIS
San Francisco
SIERRA NEVADA
KANSAS PACIFIC R.R.
ATCHISON, TOPEKA AND SANTA FE R.R.
St. Louis
MISSOURI
CALIFORNIA
ATLANTIC AND PACIFIC R.R.
KANSAS
Los Angeles
ARIZONA TERRITORY
NEW MEXICO TERRITORY
OKLAHOMA TERR.
INDIAN TERR.
ARKANSAS
PACIFIC OCEAN
30°N
MEXICO
TEXAS
SOUTHERN PACIFIC R.R.
LOUISIANA

⚒ Mining center
— Railroad

0   300 Miles
0   300 Kilometers

N
W E
S

GULF OF MEXICO

115°W   110°W   95°W   90°W

The Chinese helped build many railroads in the U.S. West, including a line linking Chicago and Butte, Montana. Which railroad connected those two cities?

Each worker stopped for a cup and then promptly returned to work. By sunset, they had built a longer and smoother track than any crew in camp.

That evening, the regular crews were even more startled. The Chinese cooks set out kegs of warm water, and each worker soaped and rinsed himself before changing into clean clothes. At dinner time, the Chinese refused to eat the dried meat, beans, and potatoes the other workers lived on. Instead, their cooks used dried oysters, cuttlefish, bamboo sprouts, seaweed, mushrooms, and abalone—a kind of shellfish—to make dishes much like ones the men had eaten in China.

The next morning, the other workers were determined to outdo the men from China. They stepped up their speed, took fewer breaks, and cut their lunch hour in half. Still the Chinese outperformed them. Strobridge was so impressed that he asked Crocker to hire 50 more Chinese workers. Within six months, over 2,000 Chinese were on the job.

The other workers were not pleased. Calling the Chinese "Crocker's pets," they demanded that the company hire only white men. Crocker told them that he was determined to build a railroad. If they did not want to get along with the Chinese, they could leave. Within two years, the Central Pacific employed over 12,000 Chinese workers—90 percent of its entire work force.

The Central Pacific used a company to recruit Chinese workers first in California and later in China. The company even offered to advance workers the money they needed for passage to California. The workers would repay the loan in seven monthly installments from their wages. At the time, they earned $26 a month, far less than white workers but more than Chinese could get elsewhere in the United States.

TAKING ANOTHER LOOK

1. Why did Californians support the building of a transcontinental railroad?

2. Why was Crocker willing to take a chance on Chinese workers for the railroad?

3. *CRITICAL THINKING* Why do you think white railroad workers objected to the hiring of Chinese?

2 BUILDING THE GREAT IRON TRAIL

What obstacles did the Chinese have to overcome in building the railroad?

When the Chinese started to work on the Central Pacific, the railroad stretched just 40 miles [64 kilometers]. Ahead lay the most difficult parts of the job—the rugged mountains called the Sierra Nevada and the mountains and desert that lay beyond them. The Chinese soon proved they could handle the huge task.

Cliff-hanging Their first challenge was Cape Horn, the name given to a granite cliff towering over the American River. The solid wall of rock had no trails. Before workers could lay track, they would have to carve a ledge 1,400 feet [420 meters] up the side of the cliff.

One Chinese worker came to Strobridge with a suggestion. He explained that he and the other workers had grown up in the mountains of South China. His people had built roads and even fortresses on similar cliffs along the Chang Jiang (Yangtze River). Now they would like permission to use those same methods on Cape Horn. Strobridge, feeling that he had nothing to lose, agreed.

As other workers watched in disbelief, the Chinese spent their evenings weaving baskets large enough to hold several men. Crews, standing on top of the cliff, would lower the baskets over the side. Suspended in air, workers in those baskets would use hammers, chisels, and blasts of gunpowder to cut the first ledges.

All through the fall and winter, the wicker baskets bobbed against the skyline. Little by little, the men in those baskets carved a narrow ledge. Sometimes a rope would break and the men in the basket would plunge to their death. Still, by spring the Chinese had done the seemingly impossible. They had carved a trail up the side of the ravine, wide enough for four workers to walk abreast.

By the summer of 1866, there were over 6,000 Chinese workers in the company's railroad camps. They now earned $31 dollars a month and were taking on more and more of the work. They were, said the railroad's chief engineer, "becoming expert in drilling, blasting, and other rock work."

Tunneling Through Once the men had carved a path up Cape Horn, they could not rest. The highest peaks of the Sierras lay between the workers and Nevada. The railroad was now to climb 4,550 feet [1,365 meters] on a 42-mile [67-kilometer] path through Donner Pass. Workers would have to build 18 tunnels, each at least 1,000 feet [300 meters] long. They would have to fill hundreds of gullies and ravines and cut down thousands of redwood and spruce trees to build **trestles**, or bridges. Some trestles stood over 100 feet [30 meters] high and spanned anywhere from 350 to 600 feet [105 to 180 meters]. The only equipment the Chinese had were two-wheel dump carts, wheelbarrows, axes, ropes, explosives, and mules.

Crocker decided to build ten tunnels at once. The longest tunnel was the Summit, 1,659 feet [497 meters] long. Here Strobridge had his men sink a shaft 73 feet [22 meters] deep. In this way, they could work not only from both ends but also from the middle. Even working around the clock, the men took a year to complete the tunnel.

As winter approached, snow began to cover the building sites. Unwilling to wait for spring, Crocker decided to have three locomotives and supplies pulled over the mountains by hand so that work could begin on the other side. Hundreds of Chinese workers cleared a path through the snow-covered forests. Then, on log sleds greased with lard, they pulled the locomotives and other supplies up one slope and down the other.

In the meantime, other workers had dug tunnels in the snow to enable them to work through the winter. That winter was one of the coldest on record, with constant snow and subzero tem-

During winters in the Sierra Nevadas, snow drifts could be 40 feet deep, and avalanches were a constant threat to workers on the Central Pacific.

peratures. Almost half of the men were used just to keep the rail line clear of snow. By January, it was no longer possible to maintain paths from the tunnels to the camps. So for the rest of the winter, the men both lived and worked in tunnels deep beneath the snowdrifts.

On Strike! As winter turned to spring, people were saying that it would take years before the Central Pacific made it through the mountains. Crocker responded by increasing the workday from 8 hours to 10 and then to 12, and extending the workweek from 6 days to 7. In June 1867, realizing that the workers were unhappy with their hours and working conditions, he offered a raise. The Chinese would now receive $35 a month. To his surprise, they told him that it was not enough. If they did not get $40 a month and an 8-hour shift, they would strike. One morning in late June, 5,000 Chinese workers did not show up for work. "If eight hours a day is good for white men, the same is good for Chinamen," they declared.

The Central Pacific and the California newspapers claimed the strike was the work of agents from the competing Union Pacific Railroad, but it was not. The workers were simply fed up. Crocker told the workers that if they did not go back to work by Monday, he would cut off their food supplies. Virtually imprisoned in their camps in the Sierras, the men had little choice. They went back to work.

All summer, the workers rushed to finish the tunnels before the winter snows began. By November, the road was 107 miles [171 kilometers] long from Sacramento to the Summit Tunnel. There were also 24 miles [38 kilometers] of track along the eastern slopes of the mountains toward the Nevada border. Only 7 miles [11 kilometers] separated the two sections of the Central Pacific's railroad track.

Blasting Through That winter, however, was as harsh as the one the year before. When January arrived, the two sections had not yet been connected, but Crocker had confidence in the ability of the Chinese. On New Year's Day, he boasted that in 1868 crews would lay at least a mile [1.6 kilometers] of track a day. All through that winter, thousands of men living in shacks and ice caves along the eastern slope of the mountains worked frantically. Some sawed

A TRADITION OF INNOVATION

The owners of the Central Pacific never knew that many of the tools used to build their railroad had been invented by the Chinese. In the 10th century, a Chinese cook mixed several common kitchen ingredients and produced an explosion. For some reason, the unnamed cook had combined potassium nitrate, used for pickling and preserving food, with sulfur and charcoal, used for the cooking fire, and thus created blasting powder.

The Chinese also invented the wheelbarrow, which rail workers used to carry supplies and haul away debris. The harness that allowed animals to carry heavy loads also came from China. Even the stirrup used in riding horses was the work of the ancient Chinese. Each of these inventions was critical in the building of the U.S. West.

timber, while others worked on the foundation for miles of snow sheds. These huge peak-roofed wooden tunnels would be the company's only hope of keeping the railroad open through the winter months.

By June, the two parts of the railroad touched, linking Sacramento to Reno, Nevada. Now the Chinese faced new obstacles. They had reached the desert—a land where the days were brutally hot and the nights numbingly cold. It was also a land where wood, coal, food, and even water had to be transported over long distances. Still, the terrain was relatively flat and therefore the pace quickened. By year's end, the workers had built 350 miles [560 kilometers] of track. As they pushed eastward, they moved closer and closer to the Utah border and to workers from the Union Pacific Railroad.

The Race Is On! As the two railroads came closer together, tensions mounted. Each side was determined to complete as much track as possible before the two lines came together at Promontory Point, Utah. If the Union Pacific laid 4 miles [6.4 kilometers] of track in a day, the Central Pacific was determined to lay 6 [9.6]. After the Union

Pacific laid 8 miles [12.8 kilometers] of track in one day, Crocker bet his rivals $10,000 that his men could do 10 [16].

At 7 A.M. on April 28, 1869, a locomotive whistle gave a long blast and the race was on. A group of Chinese workers began unloading rails, spikes, bolts, and gear from 16 flatcars. Then a group of workers lined up the ties. Next came the tracklayers, all of whom were Irish. Then a group of Chinese workers put metal plates and spikes next to each rail. Another group bolted the plates and drove in the spikes. Then track levelers lifted each rail and shoveled enough dirt under it to keep it level. Finally, tampers made sure the rails were solidly set.

When the whistle blew at 7 P.M., Crocker had won the bet. His men had completed 10 miles and 56 feet [16 kilometers] of track. They had lifted 125 tons of steel and used 25,800 wooden ties, 3,520 rails, 28,160 spikes, and 14,080 bolts and still had time for lunch.

Celebration in Utah Two weeks later, on May 10, 1869, the transcontinental railroad was finally completed. The heads of the two railroad companies were supposed to drive the last spikes, which were made of gold and silver. The workers were amused to discover that neither man was able to hit the spike even once. The Chinese had to finish the job themselves.

As the last spike went in, a telegrapher clicked the news to waiting operators all over the country. Chicago held a parade, and church chimes rang out in New York. In Philadelphia, the Liberty Bell pealed, and in San Francisco, fire bells went off. In towns and cities all along the railroad line, there were fireworks and parades. Only one person noted the role of the Chinese in building the railroad. At a speech in Sacramento, Charles Crocker told the guests:

> In the midst of our rejoicing, I wish to call to
> mind that the early completion of this railroad
> we have built has been in great measure due to
> that poor destitute [needy] class of laborers called
> the Chinese, to the fidelity [loyalty] and industry
> they have shown—and the great amount of labor-
> ers of this land that have been employed upon
> the work.

On to New Jobs Throughout the 1870s, the Chinese went on to similar work on dozens of other railroads. They helped build almost every railroad in the U.S. West and many in the South as well. When the work was done, some

When the railroad lines met at Promontory Point, this Central Pacific track crew posed for a photograph next to a box car belonging to the rival Union Pacific.

stayed on in the towns and cities that sprang up along the rail lines to start small businesses or to work in laundries or as cooks or gardeners.

One Chinese worker used his experience to build a railroad in Guangdong. His name was Chin Gee Hee. He had come to the United States in the 1860s to work on the railroad. In 1905, he returned home and built the only railroad in China entirely designed, financed, and built by Chinese. He got the money from fellow rail workers in the United States. They invested their savings in the line so that their families would prosper and their villages grow.

TAKING ANOTHER LOOK

1. What skills did the Chinese develop building the railroad?
2. Why were workers able to lay more track in 1868 than in previous years?
3. *CRITICAL THINKING* Read Crocker's comments about the Chinese on page 42. How do they suggest his opinion of Chinese workers had changed since 1865?

CHAPTER 3: CLOSE UP

KEY IDEAS

1 Linking East and West

- A transcontinental railroad was needed to link territories and states in the western United States with states in the east.
- In 1862, Congress passed the Pacific Railroad Act, which authorized the building of a rail line that would link the Atlantic and Pacific coasts.
- The Central Pacific Railroad had the right to build east from Sacramento and the Union Pacific, to build west from Omaha.
- The Central Pacific faced a labor shortage until it began to recruit Chinese workers.

2 Building the Great Iron Trail

- The Chinese applied many traditional Chinese methods to the task of building the railroad.
- Workers on the Central Pacific were challenged not only by the rugged Sierra Nevada but also by the weather.
- Chinese workers went on strike to protest low wages, long hours, and poor working conditions, but did not succeed in their efforts.
- As the Central Pacific and the Union Pacific reached Utah, competition between the two lines increased sharply.
- The transcontinental railroad was completed on May 10, 1869.
- The Chinese went on to build other railroads in the U.S. West and in China as well.

WHO, WHAT, WHERE

1. **What** was the Pacific Railroad Act?
2. **Where** did the Central Pacific Railroad begin?
3. **Where** did the Union Pacific Railroad begin?
4. **Where** did the two railroads meet?
5. **What** did the Chinese do to conquer Cape Horn?
6. **What** is a trestle?
7. **Who** won the bet Charles Crocker made in April of 1869?

8. **What** happened on May 10, 1869?

9. **What** did the Chinese do after they finished the transcontinental railroad?

UNDERSTANDING THE CHAPTER

1. Why do you think so many Chinese were willing to work on the railroad even though it was a difficult and dangerous job?

2. How did traditional ways help Chinese workers build the railroad?

3. Why did the strike that the Chinese called fail?

4. Why did General William T. Sherman call the building of a transcontinental railroad "a work of giants?

MAKING CONNECTIONS

1. What was the connection between the California gold rush and the building of a transcontinental railroad?

2. What was the connection between railroad building in the United States and the building of a railroad in Guangdong?

WRITING ABOUT HISTORY

1. Use your imagination to write a short story describing what it must have been like to work on the transcontinental railroad. Your story might focus on one winter in the Sierras or what it was like to dangle in a basket as you carved a ledge in the side of Cape Horn. Or you may wish to describe the race to lay 10 miles [16 kilometers] of track in a single day.

2. In 1969, the United States celebrated the 100th anniversary of the transcontinental railroad. Many Chinese Americans traveled to Promontory Point to attend a special ceremony. To their dismay, the U.S. Secretary of Transportation did not even mention the contribution their ancestors had made. Imagine that you also attended the event. Write a letter that would help the Secretary understand why the Chinese Americans were offended.

PIONEERS FROM CHINA

THINKING ABOUT THE CHAPTER

How did the Chinese expand their opportunities in the late 19th century?

When most people think of pioneers venturing into unknown territory, they picture 19th-century settlers moving west across the Great Plains in covered wagons to begin new lives in what would become the western United States. But not all pioneers were westward bound in the 1800s. The Chinese were pioneers who traveled east in ships, on the railroads they helped to build, and, sometimes, by foot.

Pioneers are often **innovators**, people who come up with new ideas or are among the first to try new ways of doing things. The Chinese were pioneers in this sense, too. The son of one of these pioneers said of his father and other such Chinese Americans:

SECTIONS

1 Making the Most of Opportunities

2 New Fields, New Opportunities

3 Women in a World of Men

> They started everything, you know. Oh, a lot of things in agriculture, in farming. . . . When they started fishing shrimp, you know, they got their nets from China. The Americans said, "Those Chinese are really able to do a lot of things we never thought of!"

Who were these pioneers? As you read in Chapter 2, some were sojourners, who came to the United States to make their fortune and then return home. But by the late 1800s, many more were people who had come to the United States to stay. Most were men, but increasingly, these pioneers from China included women.

By 1880, Chinese made up 50 to 75 percent of agricultural workers in some parts of California. These Chinese are harvesting a vineyard in San Marino.

1 MAKING THE MOST OF OPPORTUNITIES

How did the Chinese use traditional skills to improve farming in the United States?

In the late 1800s, the only jobs open to Chinese in the United States were jobs no one else wanted. Yet time after time, some Chinese found ways to turn dead-end jobs into new opportunities. Farm work is a good example of this.

Turning Swampland Into Farmland In 1850, the San Joaquin and Sacramento river valleys in northern California were little more than swamp, but there was rich soil beneath the standing water. Some business people bought up the wetlands for as little as $1 an acre and then hired workers to drain the marshes so they could plant crops. Almost all of these workers were Chinese.

By 1876, over 3,000 Chinese labored to turn swamplands along the Sacramento River into farmland. These workers are building a levee to hold back the river.

Using only shovels and wheelbarrows, the Chinese built levees and dikes to hold back the rivers, and miles of irrigation ditches to channel water to the fields. They often worked waist-deep in water, as they transformed 250,000 acres [100,000 hectares] of swamp into one of the richest farming regions in the United States. The top wages for these workers were $1 a day.

Because of these Chinese laborers, land that had cost $1 an acre was soon worth over $100 an acre. When the work was done, some Chinese found jobs harvesting crops on the land they had reclaimed. By the 1870s, three out of every four farmworkers in California were Chinese.

Renting Land Farmworkers earned very little, but some were able to save enough to become **tenant farmers**. A tenant farmer gives the landlord a share of the crop in exchange for the use of the land and tools, and help in selling the harvest. Those who could not afford to rent land on their own banded together to form companies known as *yuen*. Members were collectively responsible for leasing and running a farm. One of these tenant farmers was called Ah Lung.

Ah Lung came to the United States at the age of 19 with no money and very little education. Yet he was confident that if he worked hard enough in the Land of the Gold

Mountain, he would succeed. He first found work at Sing Kee, a Chinese-owned company that sold rice and other goods to Chinese workers throughout the U.S. West. At Sing Kee, the young immigrant earned $1 a day plus board, for threshing and bagging rice. Yet a single sack of rice sold for $6. Clearly, the people who made money were not those who bagged the rice but those who owned the business.

Determined that someday he, too, would own a business, Ah Lung prepared by spending his evenings studying English. The knowledge of English that he gained led to his first business opportunity. A group of men from his home district in China was planning to lease farmland near Sacramento, but none of them spoke English. They invited Ah Lung to join the company they were forming and act as interpreter.

The farm that the tiny company built prospered, and Ah Lung saved every cent he could from his share of the profits. He then invested that money in other businesses, including Sing Kee. By the time he was 30 years old, he had enough money to return to China to marry, and to bring his new wife back to the United States.

The Potato King With his wife's assistance, Ah Lung's business ventures grew. Within a few years, he was leasing over 1,000 acres [400 hectares] of farmland on his own. He specialized in growing potatoes and did so well with the crop that other farmers began to call him "the potato king."

Although he was financially successful, Ah Lung remained a tenant farmer. It was not until the late 1800s that he and his wife had saved enough money to buy a farm. By then, events in California and the nation made Ah Lung's dream of owning his own land more difficult to realize.

As you will read in Chapter 5, prejudice against the Chinese had increased during the 1870s. In 1882, the United States passed a law stating that Chinese could not become citizens. California then passed the Alien Land Act, which said that only those who could become citizens could own land in the state. Despite the setback, Ah Lung refused to give up his dream.. He purchased 2,000 acres [800 hectares] for a farm near Klamath Falls, Oregon, instead.

Ah Lung had become successful beyond his wildest dreams, but he was fearful that he would lose everything if

Oregon passed an alien land act like California's. So he decided to invest in businesses that he believed neither state nor federal government could take away.

He started an import-export business and a luggage factory in San Francisco and also opened a branch of Sing Kee in Sacramento. By now, he was earning as much as $90,000 a year—at a time when a person who earned even $3,000 a year was considered well-to-do. But his wealth could not protect him or his family from discrimination.

In 1923, Oregon passed a law similar to California's. Soon after that, Ah Lung began buying land in China. In time, he turned over his U.S. businesses to his sons, who were born in California, and returned to China.

TAKING ANOTHER LOOK

1. How did tenant farming work?
2. How did Ah Lung use the tenant farming system to open new opportunities for his family in the United States?
3. *CRITICAL THINKING* What connection do you see between the discrimination Ah Lung encountered and the way he managed his fortune?

2 NEW FIELDS, NEW OPPORTUNITIES

What new skills did the Chinese develop in the late 19th century?

Chinese pioneers looked for many types of business opportunities in the United States. In the late 19th century, they built businesses in tiny villages, boom towns, and thriving cities all across the nation. Many lived far from other Chinese and few could afford to bring their families from China to their new homes. A Guangzhou folk song expresses the loneliness of these pioneers:

> Pitiful is the 20-year sojourner,
>   unable to make it home.
> Having been everywhere—north, south, east,
>   west—

Always obstacles along the way,
    pain knitting my brows.
Worried in silence.
Ashamed, wishes unfulfilled,
A reflection in the mirror, a
    sudden fright: hair,
    half frost-white
Frequent letters from home,
    all filled with much complaint.

Chinese Laundries By the late 1800s, many Chinese regarded opening a laundry as their best opportunity to own a business of their own. As early as 1851, a man named Wah Lee set up the first Chinese "wash-house establishment" in San Francisco. By 1870, there were nearly 3,000 Chinese laundry workers in California alone. Twenty years later, their number in the state had more than doubled, and there were many in other states as well. Yet Lee Chew, who came to the United States in the 1860s, wrote:

> The Chinese laundryman does not learn his
> trade in China; there are no laundries in China.
> The women there do the washing in tubs and
> have no washboards or flat irons. All the Chinese
> laundrymen [in the United States] were taught in
> the first place by American women just as I was
> taught.

Wong Sing stands in front of his Fort Duchesne store with two customers from the Ute reservation in this photograph from early in the 1900s.

Another Chinese immigrant agreed. Wong Chin Foo wrote in 1888 that laundry work in China was a "woman's occupation" and men did not enter it for fear of "losing their social standing." Why then did Chinese men enter the laundry business in the United States? Unlike most businesses, a laundry could be started with relatively little money. All a person needed was a room with a stove, a washtub, some soap, an iron, and a sign.

Most laundries had two workers, one to do the washing and the other the ironing. The washing began about 7 A.M. on Monday morning and ended on Friday night. The washer got the weekend off. The ironing began on Tuesday and ended on Saturday, so the ironer had Sundays and Mondays off. As Chew noted, "Each works only five days a week, but those are long days—from seven o'clock in the morning until midnight."

Author L. C. Tsung described the life of a Chinese laundryman in his novel *The Marginal Man*. In the book, a character named Charles Lin asks the laundryman how long he has lived in the United States. The characters are fictional, but the situation described was common:

"Forty years," the old man answered in Cantonese and raised four fingers. . . .

"Do you have a family?"

"Big family. A woman, many sons and grandsons. All back home in Tangshan."

"Have you ever gone back since you came out here?"

"No, I only send money," replied the old man. From underneath the counter he brought out a photograph and showed it to Charles. In the center sat a white-haired old woman, surrounded by some fifteen or twenty men, women, and children of various ages. . . .

Charles Lin realized that his picture was the old man's only comfort and relaxation. He had toiled like a beast of burden for forty years to support a large family which was his aim of existence, the sole meaning of his life. The picture to him was like a diploma. . . . Behind the facade [mask] of sadness and resignation there was the inner satisfaction which made this old man's life bearable and meaningful.

Storekeeping Some Chinese in the U.S. West became peddlers, selling small articles, dishes, pots, and pans as they moved from place to place. When they found a good location, they sometimes settled down and opened a store. Wong Sing, who settled in Fort Duchesne, Utah, is one person who followed this pattern.

When Wong Sing died in 1934, no one remembered exactly how he had come to Fort Duchesne. Some thought that an officer stationed at the nearby army post had brought him to town to work as a handyman. Still others thought he had come on his own. They agreed only that he had started doing laundry at the army post in 1889.

Wong saved the money he earned washing and ironing for the soldiers. With it, he bought china and other household supplies that he sold to settlers in Utah. With his profits, he started a restaurant and later built a small store on a nearby reservation for Native Americans.

Wong encouraged the Ute [YOOT] people on the reservation to shop at his store by treating them fairly and by learning their language. Other merchants resented the competition and managed to get the U.S. government to force him off the reservation. He then built a new store just off the reservation. The Ute continued to shop there, as did ranchers and farmers from miles around.

In time, Wong employed as many as eight clerks in his shop. When he got too old to work, his son came from China to help him. After Wong's death, his son remained in Utah to run the family business.

Moving Eastward Not every Chinese storekeeper was as successful as Wong. Most earned just barely enough to survive. In their search for good places to live and work, some Chinese moved farther east.

Among them was Wong On. He had run away from his home in China when he was just 13 years old and worked his way across the United States—first as a water boy, then as a laborer—on various railroads, ending up in New Orleans. In 1875, he boarded a steamboat with a group of friends to pick cotton in the Mississippi Delta.

The young men pooled their earnings so that they could rent land and grow their own cotton. They quickly discovered what African Americans there already knew. Cotton-growing brought profits to the owners of the land; the tenant farmers barely survived. So the Chinese earned extra money by peddling candy, cloth, and other items. In time, they made enough to dissolve their partnership so that each man could go out on his own.

Wong On, like most of his friends, stayed in Mississippi, not to farm but to open a store. Later he married an African American woman. His friends already had wives and children back in China, and some could now afford to bring them to the United States.

TAKING ANOTHER LOOK

1. Why did many Chinese Americans open laundries?

2. How did some Chinese manage to become storekeepers?

3. *CRITICAL THINKING* What does Tsung mean when he writes, "The picture to him was like a diploma . . . ?" Why was the old man so proud of the picture?

3 WOMEN IN A WORLD OF MEN

How did some Chinese women break with tradition to become pioneers in the United States?

According to tradition, when a Chinese woman married, she left her home and went to live with her husband and his family. She was expected to obey not only her husband but also her parents-in-law. In China, few women traveled far from home.

In many Chinese families, women were physically unable to walk far or stand for very long. In those days, some families bound their daughters' feet to keep them from growing more than a few inches long. Small feet were considered a sign of beauty. They were also a status symbol—only a well-to-do family could afford to bind the feet of its daughters. After all, a girl with bound feet could not possibly work in the fields. Yet despite

Traditionally, daughters in Chinese families did not receive formal education. The single girl in this 1890 California public school class was an exception.

FLORIDA ORANGES

When people think of oranges, they often think of Florida. The two are closely linked because the citrus industry helped the state prosper and grow. Yet oranges are not native to Florida. They originated in China over 4,000 years ago. The fruit came to Florida by way of Spain, but the plants did not flourish. The orange trees died as soon as the weather turned cold.

Then, in the late 1800s, Lue Gim Gong settled in De Land, Florida. He was an immigrant from China, who had worked in a shoe factory in North Adams, Massachusetts. His Sunday school teacher there had taught him English and encouraged his interest in plants and gardening. When he developed tuberculosis, she offered him a house and a little land in Florida. There, as he regained his strength, he began to experiment with oranges.

Lue bred various kinds of orange trees until he found one that both produced juicy fruit and resisted frost. Without his new variety of orange, Florida would have had no citrus industry. In 1911, the United States Department of Agriculture recognized his contribution to the citrus industry by giving Lue the Wilder Medal, its highest honor.

bound feet and a family structure that kept women close to home, some Chinese women broke with tradition and came to the United States.

Gold Mountain Widows A Chinese woman who married a sojourner often had more money than her neighbors, but she was also lonelier than they. Most of these "Gold Mountain widows," as they were known, raised their children alone. They lived only briefly with their husbands before the men went off to make their fortunes.

A few women refused to stay at home and wait for their husbands to send them money. In 1869, a writer told of "a wife coming all the way alone across the stormy sea" to be with her husband:

Friends at home besought [begged] her not to do a thing so in conflict with Chinese custom; the husband and his relatives in this country, when they heard of her purpose, wrote entreating her not to expose herself to the hardships and perils of the sea, and to the trials which would be liable to befall her here; but she answered that where the husband was, there she had a right to be.

In California, she earned an income sewing and making cigarettes, while her husband worked for a mining company.

One woman came to the United States only to find herself virtually imprisoned in the laundry her husband owned. She was able to leave the business only three times in 38 years. Other women were equally isolated. They had no opportunity to learn English or even to visit with family and friends. One Chinese American, who grew up in Sebastopol, California, wrote of the settlement there, "Well, there they were three hundred of them [Chinese] . . . and except for my mother, not a single woman."

A Woman of Independence It took courage for a Chinese woman to join her husband in the United States. It took even more courage for an unmarried woman to emigrate. Yet a number of single women came to the United States in the late 1800s. Among them was Yun Oi, who had become a widow during her first year of marriage. Childless and unhappy in the home of her dead husband's family, she decided to strike out on her own.

First, Yun Oi went to Guangzhou to look for work. Then, in the late 1870s, she had the chance to travel to the United States with a relative. Soon after they arrived in the United States, he went on to New York, while Yun Oi stayed in San Francisco.

In San Francisco, her clan helped her find work as a bride escort. She helped prepare brides for their weddings and then accompanied them in the wedding procession. It was an honorable occupation for a woman in China, but there were too few Chinese women in California for a bride escort to prosper. So Yun Oi supplemented her income by taking in sewing and working as a hairdresser, and invested her earnings in other businesses.

Thirty years later, Yun Oi had earned enough to return to Guangzhou in style. By then, she had enough money to adopt several children and to buy not only a business but also property that she then leased out to tenants.

A Woman of the Sea Most Chinese women in the United States followed traditional occupations. They sewed, farmed, or helped in family businesses. But in the far north, in what is now the state of Alaska, one woman did not live a traditional life in any sense of the word.

At the turn of the century, Mary Bong made a living fishing for salmon in an 18-foot [5.5-meter] open boat. She would get up at dawn, fish all day, and then come home to sell her catch. Fishing was not a new job for her. She was a Tanka, one of the boat people of southeastern China. When she was 6, her parents had been forced to go ashore to look for farm work. The family stripped the leaves from mulberry trees, picked oranges, or harvested rice. It was not the life the girl wanted, so she ran away from home.

Mary Bong found work in a port city and saved her money. She wanted to save enough to come to the United States. However, in those days, the United States required that Chinese women who wished to immigrate prove that they were of "correct habits and good character." Even those who had such proof were sometimes turned away or held in San Francisco and other ports of entry for months. So Mary decided to go to Vancouver, Canada, instead.

There, Mary Bong married a man who owned a restaurant in Sitka, then the capital of the Alaska Territory. She was perhaps the only Chinese woman in all of Alaska. She had learned enough English to run her husband's restaurant, but he died and she lost the restaurant. To support her two daughters, she became a housekeeper.

Several years later, Mary Bong remarried. Her second husband, Fred Johnson, was not the kind of man to settle in one place. She enrolled her daughters in a boarding school so that they could receive a good education, and then joined her husband in the kind of adventures that most women of her time never experienced.

When gold was discovered in Alaska in 1899, Mary Bong went to the gold fields. Her husband taught her how to dig for gold and use blasting powder. When she smashed

This photograph of Mary Bong was taken in the early years of the 20th century.

a finger in a mining accident, she sewed up the wound herself and went back to work.

Later she and her husband started a dairy at Sawmill Creek, near Sitka. In time, the couple gave up the dairy and again tried prospecting for gold and, later, trapping. When a cannery opened, fishing became Sitka's main industry. Many local Chinese sought indoor jobs at the cannery, but Mary Bong preferred to work outdoors, fishing from her boat.

At the age of 70, Mary Bong was working as a matron at the federal jail in Sitka. When asked if she would ever return to China, she said, "I'll never go back, China seems like a faraway dream to me." For her, as for many other Chinese who had come to work in the Land of the Gold Mountain, the United States had become home.

TAKING ANOTHER LOOK

1. Why were many Chinese women reluctant to live in the United States?

2. What opportunities did Mary Bong find in the United States?

3. *CRITICAL THINKING* Why were women who married sojourners known as Gold Mountain widows?

CHAPTER 4: CLOSE UP

KEY IDEAS

1 Making the Most of Opportunities

- Chinese workers turned swampland in the San Joaquin and Sacramento river valleys into some of the richest farmland in the United States.
- By the 1870s, three out of every four farm workers in California were Chinese.
- Tenant farming offered the Chinese an opportunity to get ahead.
- Laws prohibiting Chinese from owning land in California and Oregon made it difficult for them to prosper through farming. Therefore, some Chinese looked for new opportunities in other businesses.

2 New Fields, New Opportunites

- By the late 1800s, many Chinese owned or worked in laundries.
- Some Chinese became peddlers and storekeepers.
- In their search for good places to live and work, some Chinese moved further east.

3 Women in a World of Men

- A few Chinese women broke with tradition and left home to come to the United States.
- In the late 1800s, a small number of single Chinese women came to the United States.
- Most Chinese women in the United States followed traditional occupations, such as sewing, farming, or helping in family businesses, but others worked in occupations that were new to them..

WHO, WHAT, WHERE

1. **What** is an innovator?
2. **Where** did the Chinese reclaim farmland in the 1850s?
3. **What** was a *yuen*?
4. **What** was the Alien Land Act?
5. **Who** was Ah Lung?
6. **Who** was Wong Sing?

7. **What** was a Gold Mountain widow?

8. **Who** was Yun Oi?

9. **Who** was Mary Bong?

UNDERSTANDING THE CHAPTER

1. How did the tenant farming system provide opportunities for Chinese immigrants?

2. Why did many Chinese immigrants become involved in the laundry business?

3. Why did some Chinese pioneers move from the U.S. West to states in the South?

4. Why did it take courage for Chinese women to come to the United States?

MAKING CONNECTIONS

1. What was the connection between the way the Chinese organized and cooperated—in forming *yuen*, for example—and their successes in business?

2. What was the connection between the fact that many Chinese men came as sojourners and the fact that there were a small number of Chinese women in the United States in the mid–1800s?

3. What was the connection between the mining industry in California and the growth of Chinese laundries?

WRITING ABOUT HISTORY

1. Write an article that could have appeared in a California newspaper announcing the completion of the Sacramento River valley swamp reclamation project that the Chinese worked on.

2. Imagine you are a Chinese tenant farmer who has saved enough money to buy your own land. Write a letter to the governor of California protesting the Alien Land Act.

3. Imagine you are a Chinese laundry worker. Write a letter to your family in China explaining why you have chosen that occupation.

CHAPTER

5

THE DOORS SHUT

THINKING ABOUT THE CHAPTER

Why did restrictions on the rights of the Chinese in the United States increase in the late 1800s?

I n 1868, the Chinese Six Companies—the association that acted as the government of San Francisco's Chinatown—had reason to celebrate. The United States and China had just signed a new treaty. Thanks to the efforts of the Six Companies, the Burlingame Treaty, as it was known, protected the rights of Chinese immigrants.

When Chinese American leaders first learned that a treaty was being worked on, they contacted a San Francisco lawyer involved in the negotiations. They persuaded him and others of the need for a clause protecting the Chinese in the United States and their property. To their delight, in the final agreement, the governments of China and the United States recognized the right of the Chinese people to "free migration and emigration" to the United States as visitors, traders, and "permanent residents." In addition, the treaty promised the Chinese "the same privileges, immunities [freedoms], and exemptions in respect to travel or residence" in the United States as citizens or subjects of other nations.

SECTIONS

1 Discrimination in California

2 Answering the "Chinese Question"

3 After Exclusion

62

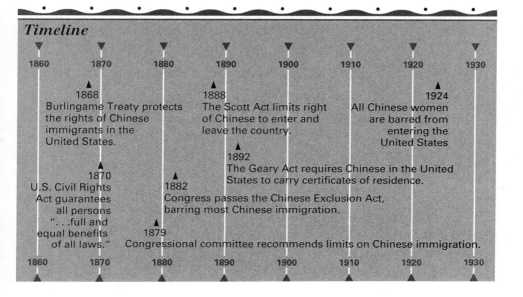

Timeline

1860	1870	1880	1890	1900	1910	1920	1930

1868
Burlingame Treaty protects the rights of Chinese immigrants in the United States.

1888
The Scott Act limits right of Chinese to enter and leave the country.

1924
All Chinese women are barred from entering the United States

1892
The Geary Act requires Chinese in the United States to carry certificates of residence.

1870
U.S. Civil Rights Act guarantees all persons "...full and equal benefits of all laws."

1882
Congress passes the Chinese Exclusion Act, barring most Chinese immigration.

1879
Congressional committee recommends limits on Chinese immigration.

No other immigrants turned to treaties to protect their rights. Why did the Chinese? The answer lies, in part, in the attitudes and beliefs that marked U.S. society in the 19th century. It was a time when many white Americans regarded themselves as superior to other groups. Slavery did not end in the United States until 1865, just three years before the treaty was signed. Even after slavery ended, many whites in both the North and the South continued to **discriminate** against African Americans, or treat them unjustly because of their race. They also discriminated against Native Americans and Hispanics. Many white Americans were also hostile to immigrants arriving from Europe.

As the first free nonwhite immigrants, the Chinese were far more vulnerable to discrimination than other newcomers. Unlike other immigrants, they could not become citizens. In 1790, Congress had passed a law that allowed only free white immigrants to apply for citizenship. That law was still in effect in 1868.

The Burlingame Treaty did not end discrimination against the Chinese. In fact, discrimination increased greatly in the years after it was signed. In this chapter, you will find out why that happened and how it affected the Chinese.

1 DISCRIMINATION IN CALIFORNIA

What kinds of discrimination did the Chinese experience in California?

California was the first place in the United States where immigrants from China settled, and it was where most of them lived in the 1800s. It was also the place where anti-Chinese feeling was the strongest. The Six Companies there (see page 28) had been fighting prejudice for a long time with only a little success.

Fighting for Legal Protection The Six Companies realized that the 1868 Burlingame Treaty was just one victory in what would be a long war against discrimination. In 1869, Chinese merchants met in San Francisco with a group of congressional representatives. The Chinese told the lawmakers of the need for federal laws to ensure the equal protection guaranteed in the treaty. Pointing to measures like the foreign miners' tax (see page 25), one merchant argued, "We are willing to pay taxes cheerfully, when taxed equally with others." He went on to say:

> Most of all—we feel the want of protection to life and property when Courts of Justice refuse our testimony, and thus leave us defenseless, and unable to obtain justice for ourselves.

The Chinese merchant was referring to a California Supreme Court ruling. In 1853, George W. Hall had been tried for the murder of a Chinese man. Four witnesses testified against Hall—one was white, and the other three, Chinese. After hearing the testimony, a jury convicted Hall.

Hall's lawyer appealed the case to the state supreme court. There, he argued that the verdict was based mainly on the testimony of the Chinese witnesses, who, according to California law, could not testify against whites. The lawyer was referring to an 1850 statute that stated "no black, or Mulatto person, or Indian shall be allowed to give evidence in favor of, or against a white person."

The state supreme court acquitted Hall. The judges accepted the lawyer's argument that since the Chinese came from Asia, once known to Europeans as the Indies, they

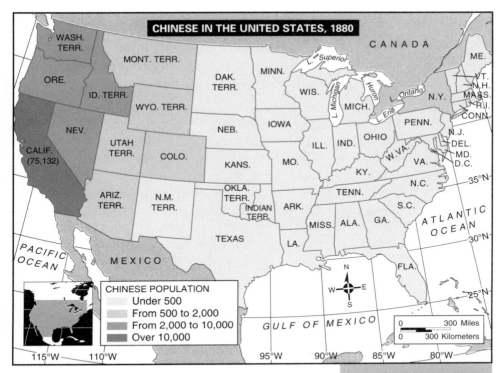

CHINESE IN THE UNITED STATES, 1880

CHINESE POPULATION
- Under 500
- From 500 to 2,000
- From 2,000 to 10,000
- Over 10,000

CALIF. (75,132)

In what part of the United States had the largest number of Chinese settled by 1880? What state had the largest number of Chinese?

were "Indians." The judges went on to say that even if the law did not apply, they would *still* have ruled against the right of the Chinese to testify. After all, if the Chinese could testify, they would soon have "all the equal rights of citizenship, and we might soon see them at the polls, in the jury box, upon the bench and in the legislative halls."

Federal laws passed after the Hall ruling did seem to offer the Chinese some protection. The Civil Rights Act of 1870 stated that "all persons" within the jurisdiction of the United States have the same right "to the full and equal benefit of all laws and proceedings for the security of person and property as is enjoyed by white citizens . . . any law . . . to the contrary notwithstanding."

Laws, however, are meaningful only when they are enforced, and the Civil Rights Act was not enforced in California. Just two years after it was passed, author Mark Twain wrote:

> Any white man can swear a Chinaman's life away in the courts, but no Chinaman can testify

against a white man. Ours is "the land of the free"—nobody denies that—nobody challenges it. (Maybe it is because we won't let other people testify.)

A Time of Violence and Fear The 1870s were difficult years in the United States. The nation was in the midst of a **depression**, a severe economic decline. Many businesses failed and jobs were hard to find. In California, the years of quick money in mining were over. Yet more and more people were coming every year—all looking for work. As a result, the competition for jobs was intense. A popular song suggests common attitudes toward the Chinese:

O workingmen dear, and did you hear
The news that's goin' around?
Another China steamer
Has been landed here in town.
Today I read the papers,
And it grieved my heart full sore
To see upon the title page,
"O, just Twelve Hundred More!"
O California's coming down,
As you can plainly see.
They are hiring all the Chinamen
and discharging you and me. . . .

Were the Chinese a threat? The Chinese Six Companies argued that they were not. "Up to 800,000 Europeans enter the United States per year, yet the labor unions hardly cared." But, the group noted, "A few thousands of the Chinese arrivals would irritate American workers."

Chinese leaders also responded to charges that Chinese workers took jobs from whites by working for lower wages. "Our labor was 'never cheap' and 'always commanded the highest market price.'" wrote Lee Chew, a laundryman. He blamed the charge on "the jealousy of laboring men of other nationalities."

State lawmakers paid little attention to such arguments. After all, the Chinese could not vote, but the men who attacked them could and *did* vote. From 1870 on, almost every candidate in the state ran on an anti-Chinese platform. Political parties in the state competed to pass anti-Chinese legislation. Speeches by politicians stirred up

Signs in background: CHINAMEN FOR ALL WORK | CHINESE NURSES | OFFICE FOR CHINESE SERVANTS | CHINESE LAUNDRY OF SAM LEE

feelings of anger in unemployed workers that sometimes exploded in anti-Chinese riots during the 1870s.

Politicians also enacted state laws restricting immigration. In 1870, for example, a California law required immigrants born in China, Japan, or islands nearby either to post a **bond**—a sum of money guaranteeing good behavior—or to prove that they were "of good character." Immigrants from other nations were not required to do the same.

City politicians, too, tried to harass the Chinese. The San Francisco Board of Supervisors openly admitted that it hoped to "drive [the Chinese] to other states" and to discourage other Chinese from moving to the city. One of the laws it passed was known as the Cubic Air Ordinance. It required 500 cubic feet [10 cubic meters] of air for each person living in a tenement, or apartment building, but it was enforced only in Chinatown. City officials did not arrest the landlords who crowded too many people into a single building, but rather the Chinese who rented the rooms.

Challenging the Laws The Chinese fought back by challenging discriminatory laws in court. The Six Companies hired prominent white attorneys, and those lawyers took a number of cases all the way to the U.S. Supreme Court. As a result, many of the discriminatory laws were declared unconstitutional. The court reminded California that only the federal government could regulate immigration.

This 1880s cartoon expressed fears of many white Americans that Chinese would take over their jobs. Its caption read, "How our streets will look next summer."

The Chinese also fought back with a technique that African Americans would later use in their struggle for equal rights. They resisted nonviolently, choosing to fill the jails rather than pay fines. That was how, for example, the Chinese responded to the Cubic Air Ordinance. In the end, this law was set aside by the courts.

The Chinese in California, however, had little reason to rejoice in their successes in court. Those successes did not stop prejudice and discrimination. Instead, they encouraged white Californians to look to the U.S. Congress for new laws to exclude the Chinese.

TAKING ANOTHER LOOK

1. What effect did the state supreme court ruling in the Hall case have on the Chinese in California?
2. How did the Chinese respond to laws that harassed them or limited their rights?
3. *CRITICAL THINKING* What did Twain mean when he said, "Ours is 'the land of the free'—nobody denies that— nobody challenges it. (Maybe it is because we won't let other people testify.)"?

2 ANSWERING THE "CHINESE QUESTION"

What was the "Chinese question" and how did Americans answer it in the late 1800s?

After the Civil War, people in the United States considered what was called the "Chinese question." What was to be done about immigration from China? At first, this was considered a matter mainly of interest to people in the western states, where large numbers of Chinese had settled. From 1869 on, however, a series of events led people in eastern states also to become concerned with the issue.

Cheap Labor On May 1, 1869, many New Yorkers read an article by writer Henry George in their morning newspaper. It began with these words:

The 60,000 or 100,000 Mongolians [Asians] on our Western coast are the thin edge of the wedge which has for its base the 500,000,000 of Eastern Asia. . . . The Chinaman can live where stronger than he would starve. Give him fair play and this quality enables him to drive out stronger races.

George went on to describe what came to be called "the yellow peril." It was the first of many articles, books, and pamphlets that warned Americans of the threat of a "Mongolian invasion." The danger in such an invasion was "cheap labor."

A year later, a shoe manufacturer in North Adams, Massachusetts, hired 75 Chinese to break a strike called by a labor union. The owner of the company refused to tell anyone what he paid the Chinese, but he did admit it was far less than he paid his union workers before they went on strike. The arrival of the Chinese made headlines. It seemed to be proof that George was right, that the Chinese were invading the nation.

In all, U.S. factories employed fewer than a thousand Chinese workers. Yet many U.S. workers saw those Chinese as a threat to their future. They claimed that the hiring of the Chinese was an "attempt to revive the institution of slavery." In 1870, the National Labor Union, which was made up of unions from all over the country, passed a resolution calling for an end to immigration from China.

Of Federal Concern The U.S. Congress considered Asian immigration for the first time in 1870. Two years earlier, the 14th Amendment was added to the Constitution, guaranteeing African American males the same rights other white American males enjoyed. Congress then had to revise the 1790 law limiting citizenship to free white immigrants, to allow immigrants of "African descent" to become citizens as well. Some representatives talked of including Asians in the new law also. Senator Charles Sumner of Massachusetts was among those who favored the idea, arguing that there was no "yellow peril." In his words, "the greatest peril to this republic is from disloyalty to its great ideas." His was a minority view. Asians remained "ineligible for citizenship" until after World War II.

A Matter for Investigation Throughout the 1870s, lawmakers were bombarded with mail urging them to outlaw immigration from China. In 1876, the House of Representatives and the Senate formed a committee to look into the "Chinese question." The committee went to California to study the "effect of Chinese immigration to this country."

Among those who spoke for the Chinese was Charles Crocker of the Central Pacific Railroad (see Chapter 3). So did a number of large landowners who used Chinese workers on their farms and ranches. Support for the Chinese also came from various religious groups. They praised the Chinese as hard-working people willing to take jobs white citizens did not want.

Those who spoke against the Chinese were mainly workers and politicians. They argued that the Chinese weakened U.S. standards by working for low wages—wages that no "real American" would accept. They also pointed to what they considered "strange" customs and dress as proof that the Chinese would never **assimilate**, or become a part of U.S. life. When the hearings were over, Senator Aaron A. Sargent of California spoke for the majority:

№ 44879 ORIGINAL.

UNITED STATES OF AMERICA.

Certificate of Residence.

Issued to Chinese _Person other than laborer_, under the Provisions of the Act of May 5, 1892.

This Is to Certify That _Ma Ling Dan_, a Chinese _Person other than laborer_, now residing at _____ has made application No. _____ to me for a Certificate of Residence under the provisions of the Act of Congress approved May 5, 1892, and I certify that it appears from the affidavits of witnesses submitted with said application that said _Ma Ling Dan_ was within the limits of the United States at the time of the passage of said Act, and was then residing at _____ and that he was at that time lawfully entitled to remain in the United States, and that the following is a descriptive list of said Chinese _Person other than laborer_, viz:

Name: _Ma Ling Dan_ Age: _51 yrs._
Local Residence: _____
Occupation: _____ Height: _5 ft 6¾ in._ Color of Eyes: _Brown_
Complexion: _____ Physical Marks or Peculiarities for Identification: _____

And as a further means of identification, I have affixed hereto a photographic likeness of said _Ma Ling Dan_.

Given under my hand and seal this _____ day of _February_, 1894, at _Portland_, State of _Oregon_.

_____ Collector of Internal Revenue,

District of _Oregon_

SCI. AM. N.Y.

The committee recommends that measures be taken by the Executive [presidential branch of government] toward the modification of the existing treaty with China, confining it to strictly commercial purposes; and that Congress legislate to restrain the great influx [inflow] of Asiatics to this country.

Anti-Chinese feeling in the United States led to the passage of a law that required Chinese living in this country to carry certificates of residence like the one shown here.

Exclusion The majority report confirmed what Californians already believed, and people there intensified their fight against the Chinese. A new state constitution in 1878 made it illegal for anyone to employ the Chinese. No corporation could hire them, nor could any state, city, or town government. Other states began to model their own anti-Chinese laws after those in California.

The U.S. government also moved against the Chinese. By 1881, the nation had a new treaty with China. It gave the U.S. government the right to "regulate, limit, or suspend" the immigration of Chinese laborers. However, the treaty did protect the right of teachers, students, merchants, and wealthy tourists to come to the United States.

In 1882, Congress passed a law known as the Chinese Exclusion Act. It stated that no Chinese worker, skilled or unskilled, could come to the United States for a period of ten years. Chinese already in the United States could stay, and the law protected their right to enter and leave the country freely. If they wished to visit China, all they had to do was get a certificate before they left, as evidence of their right to return. Many Americans believed that the "Chinese question" had been answered.

TAKING ANOTHER LOOK

1. What arguments did those who opposed Chinese immigration use?
2. What arguments did those who favored immigration use?
3. *CRITICAL THINKING* What did Charles Sumner mean when he said "the greatest peril to this republic" was not from the Chinese but "from disloyalty to its great ideas"?

3 AFTER EXCLUSION

How did the Exclusion Act affect the way the Chinese lived and worked in the United States?

In the years after the Exclusion Act was passed, it became clear that the "Chinese question" had not been settled. Acts of violence against Chinese Americans increased dramatically. The most serious violence was in the western United States. There were riots not only in California but also in places like Denver, Colorado, and Rock Springs, Wyoming. The Chinese were forcibly expelled from Seattle and Tacoma, Washington and Portland, Oregon.

A Growing Hostility The violence had little to do with any threat posed by the Chinese. Denver had only 450 Chinese in a city of about 40,000. Those workers were not a great economic threat, since most of them were employed

In 1885, white miners in Rock Springs , Wyoming Territory, attacked their Chinese coworkers, killing 28 and driving hundreds of others out of the town.

in Chinese laundries. The riots had more to do with prejudice than they did with jobs.

Some believed that the hostility grew out of the way the Chinese were pictured in books, magazines, and newspapers. They were repeatedly described as an evil people who threatened American life. It was easy for troublemakers to play on those prejudices and fears.

In many places, officials charged with upholding the laws were as prejudiced as those who broke them. A white rancher in Montana commented on the acquittal of 3 men who stood trial for the murder of 31 Chinese miners:

> I guess if they had killed 31 white men something would have been done about it, but none of the jury knew the Chinamen or knew much about it, so they turned the men loose.

Newspapers, too, often found reasons to excuse acts of violence against the Chinese. At the turn of the century, the

A DEBT OF HONOR

In March 1916, Pancho Villa, a revolutionary leader in Mexico, raided a town in New Mexico, killing 17 people. President Woodrow Wilson ordered General John J. Pershing to go to Mexico and track down Villa. Almost immediately, Pershing's army of 10,000 men found themselves in serious trouble. Their supply trucks broke down in the mountains and deserts of northern Mexico. They might have died had it not been for the help they received from a group of Chinese who lived in Mexico.

The Chinese brought Pershing's troops wagons piled high with supplies. When the Mexican government told them they could not use public highways to help the Americans, the Chinese loaded the supplies on mules and horses, or carried them on their own backs. When Pershing returned to Texas, he brought with him 527 Chinese, despite the Exclusion Act. He believed that he owed those men a debt of honor.

For the next five years, Pershing tried to get U.S. citizenship for the men. Although that effort failed, he did manage to secure permanent residence for all 527. The men settled in San Antonio, where many of their descendants live today.

Chinese ambassador responded to such excuses by asking reporters, "Why can't you be fair? Would you talk like that if mine was not a weak nation? Would you say it if the Chinese had votes?"

Tightening the Laws Against this backdrop of violence and hostility, Congress tried to shut down Chinese immigration even more thoroughly. An 1884 law outlawed Chinese immigration from non-Asian countries. In 1888, Congress passed the Scott Act, which took away the right of Chinese already in the United States to enter and leave the country freely. About 20,000 Chinese were out of the country when the law was passed. They could not return, even though they had received certificates guaranteeing that they could.

In 1892, Congress made exclusion laws even stricter. Every Chinese in the United States had to prove that he or she was in the country legally. Anyone unable to do so could be deported. This meant that every Chinese had to get a certificate of residence, a kind of internal passport. Most refused at first to obey this new law, known as the Geary Act, and some challenged it in court. The U.S. Supreme Court, however, upheld the law.

Congress continued to pass new laws through the early 1900s. Until 1924, the wives and children of Chinese merchants and American-born Chinese could still come to the United States. That year, a new immigration act went into effect. It stated that *no* Chinese woman could enter the United States to live—even if her husband and children were permitted to as U.S. citizens. Later that law was softened, but it continued to separate many families.

The Burden of Exclusion The exclusion laws and discrimination meant hardship and suffering for the Chinese in the United States. As one Chinese American writer noted:

> In every Chinese American family history there are stories of lives made miserable by the immigration laws, harassment and fear: the lonely old single men in condemned hotel rooms, the suicides of deportees, the fragmented families.

Despite these barriers, many Chinese resolved to continue their fight against discrimination and prejudice. You will learn in the next chapter how they did so and, in the process, created strong communities in the United States.

TAKING ANOTHER LOOK

1. Why did violent acts against the Chinese increase after the Exclusion Act was passed?
2. How did the laws passed after 1882 limit the rights of Chinese already in the United States?
3. *CRITICAL THINKING* A Chinese American newspaper editor called the exclusion acts "extermination acts." What did he mean by that remark?

CHAPTER 5: CLOSE UP

1 Discrimination in California

- The Burlingame Treaty, signed in 1868 by the United States and China, recognized the right of the Chinese to immigrate freely to the United States.
- In 1853, the California Supreme Court ruled that Chinese witnesses could not testify against whites, making it very difficult for Chinese to get fair trials.
- The U.S. Civil Rights Act of 1870, which stated that all persons have the same rights as white citizens, was not enforced in California.

2 Answering the "Chinese Question"

- A U.S. Congressional committee formed in 1876 to address the "Chinese question" recommended that Chinese immigration be restricted.
- California passed many anti-Chinese laws, after which other states modeled their own anti-Chinese laws.
- In 1882, Congress passed the Chinese Exclusion Act, a law stating that no Chinese worker, skilled or unskilled, could come to the United States for ten years.

3 After Exclusion

- Hostility towards Chinese increased after the Exclusion Act and resulted in outbreaks of violence directed against the Chinese.
- Through the early 1900s, Congress continued to tighten restrictions against Chinese immigration.
- Exclusion laws and discrimination meant hardship and suffering for the Chinese in the United States.

WHO, WHAT, WHERE

1. **What** was the Hall ruling?
2. **What** was the Cubic Air Ordinance?
3. **What** was the "Chinese Question?"
4. **Who** was Henry George?
5. **What** was the "yellow peril?"
6. **Where** were Chinese first hired in the United States to break a strike?

7. **Where** were Chinese forcibly "deported" from after the Exclusion Act?
8. **What** was the Geary Act?

UNDERSTANDING THE CHAPTER

1. How did Chinese leaders respond to anti-Chinese laws and discrimination?
2. Why did anti-Chinese feelings spread from the western states to other parts of the United States?
3. How did Congress attempt to resolve the "Chinese question?"
4. What effects did anti-Chinese laws and discrimination have on the Chinese?

MAKING CONNECTIONS

1. What was the connection between the economic state of the country in the 1870s and the anti-Chinese feelings of white workers?
2. What was the connection between the anti-Chinese platforms of California politicans and the fact that the Chinese could not vote?

WRITING ABOUT HISTORY

1. In 1869, merchants who were members of the Chinese Six Companies met with U.S. congressional representatives in San Francisco. Write a speech one of these merchants might have delivered explaining why the Hall ruling was unfair.
2. Write a short one-act play about the Chinese resistance to the Cubic Air Ordinance. Characters in the play might be Chinese tenants, a landlord, policemen, lawyers, and a leader of the Six Companies.
3. Imagine you are one of the Chinese workers hired to break the strike at the shoe factory in 1870. Write a letter to a friend on the West Coast discussing your situation and the anti-Chinese reaction in newspapers.

BREAKING BARRIERS

*How did the Chinese struggle
to overcome the barriers
they faced in the United States
in the late 1800s and early 1900s?*

n 1915, a Chinese American college student wrote
the following poem, expressing his hopes for what
society in the United States could be:

Let here begin a Brotherhood of man,
Wherein the West shall freely meet the
    East,
And man greet man as man.

But in 1915, the barriers to "Brotherhood" were
great. Everywhere in the nation, the Chinese faced

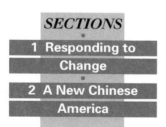

SECTIONS

**1 Responding to
Change**

**2 A New Chinese
America**

hostility, humiliation, and hardship.
They called their situation *hec fu*—
"eating bitterness." Most Chinese,
however, did not give up on the United
States or on other Americans. They
stayed and fought for the rights other
immigrants enjoyed—in particular, the
right to become U.S. citizens. They
also saw to it that their children—U.S.
citizens by birth—took full advantage of all that the
nation had to offer. In this chapter, you will learn
more about the barriers the Chinese faced after 1882
and how those obstacles affected Chinese life in the
United States.

1 RESPONDING TO CHANGE

How did life change for the Chinese in many small cities and towns in the U.S. West during the late 1800s and early 1900s?

When the Exclusion Act was passed in 1882, almost 78 percent of the Chinese in the United States lived in small towns and rural areas. These were mainly in the U.S. West, but also in the South and the Middle West. Almost every railroad town had its own Chinese community, as did most mining towns.

In Butte, Montana, for example, the Chinese made up about 20 percent of the town's population in 1880. Most of those Chinese were independent miners, who worked their own claims. Then, in 1883, the supreme court of the territory of Montana declared that the mining claims of the Chinese were invalid. The court ruled that anyone who could not become a U.S. citizen could not own a mine. Discrimination against the Chinese increased in much the same way in other towns and cities across the nation. In some places, the Chinese lost their land. In others, they lost their jobs and businesses.

Before exclusion laws took effect, Idaho had one of the largest Chinese populations in the country. This Chinese New Year parade was held in Boise in 1911.

Changes in Employment After the court's ruling, the Chinese in Butte looked for other ways of making a living. Those who had saved a little money set up laundries and restaurants that catered to white miners. Almost all other Chinese took jobs in those businesses or found work in private homes, hotels, and rooming houses as servants.

These changes were repeated across the nation in the years after the Exclusion Act was passed. Numbers tell the story better than words. In the 1870s, most Chinese were miners and railroad workers. At one time, over 12,000 Chinese worked for the Central Pacific and other rail lines. By 1920, fewer than 500 held railroad jobs, and only 150 of the 45,614 Chinese workers in the United States still worked in mines. The majority—26,488—were employed in laundries and restaurants.

Boycott! In the early 1900s, some whites in Butte and other places were not satisfied with the recent anti-Chinese laws. They wanted to drive all of the Chinese out of the country. Between 1895 and 1906, labor unions in many cities organized **boycotts** of Chinese-owned businesses. That is, members refused to do business with Chinese laundries, restaurants, and other stores. The unions also set up picket lines to keep out other customers as well.

Butte's Chinese community collected money to hire Wilbur Fisk Sanders, a former U.S. Senator, as their lawyer. Both he and his clients knew that the Chinese could not fight the boycott directly. After all, no Chinese could testify against a white person in court. So Sanders decided to see what would happen if he and a few public officials tried to enter a Chinese restaurant in Butte. When the picketers refused to let them go in, Sanders called the police. He then pressed charges against the picketers for interfering with *his* civil rights. The courts ruled in Sanders's favor, and the boycott eventually ended.

Settling In The victory did not end discrimination, but it did allow the Chinese to earn a living in Butte. Some Chinese men prospered enough to send to China for their wives and their children. After all, they were merchants now, and as merchants, they were exempt from the Exclusion Law.

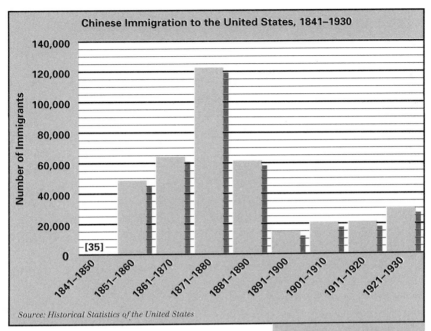

Chinese Immigration to the United States, 1841–1930

Number of Immigrants

140,000
120,000
100,000
80,000
60,000
40,000
20,000
0
[35]

1841–1850 1851–1860 1861–1870 1871–1880 1881–1890 1891–1900 1901–1910 1911–1920 1921–1930

Source: Historical Statistics of the United States

According to the graph when did Chinese immigration to the United States drop most sharply? When did the first major exclusion law take effect?

Slowly, a real Chinese community developed in the city—one with children as well as adults. At first, couples tried to live much as they had in China. But by the early 1900s, Chinese family life was changing, due, at least in part, to a revolution in China. In 1911, the Chinese people overthrew their emperor and created a republic. Most Chinese Americans supported that revolution.

The revolution in China brought with it changes in ways of life among the Chinese living in the United States. A Chinese woman in Butte recalled those changes:

> Until the [1911] Revolution, I was allowed out of the house but once a year. That was during New Years when families exchanged. . . calls and feasts. . . . After the Revolution in China, I heard that women there were free to go out. . . . I discarded my Chinese clothes and began to wear American clothes. By that time my children were going to American schools, could speak English, and they helped me buy what I needed. Gradually the other women followed my example.

One Change Leads to Others While the Chinese community in Butte was changing, the town itself was changing as well. In the past, Butte—as a newly settled town—had been a community of men. Now, it was becoming a community of families. When towns in the U.S. West had first been settled, many businesses, such as restaurants and laundries, did jobs traditionally done by women at home. They had prospered. Now, as increasing numbers of women arrived in these towns, the need for such services was not as great. As a result, Chinese laundries and restaurants in places such as Butte competed for shrinking business, and it became harder and harder for the Chinese there to make a living.

Other factors added to the difficulties that Chinese business owners faced. In the past, for example, to run a laundry required much hard work, but very few tools and other equipment. Now, however, many laundries began to use machines, which made it more expensive to run those businesses. One laundryman explained the reasons for the move to machines: "We had to do it because the immigration law restricted [laborers] from coming. Laundries were short of help."

No new Chinese were arriving in Butte, and older Chinese residents were moving out. As a result, the Chinese population of Butte shrank rapidly. In 1880, the 710 Chinese in Butte had represented 20 percent of the city's total population. By 1911—the year of China's revolution—the number of Chinese residing in Butte had dwindled to about 280, less than 1 percent of the total population. By 1940, Butte's Chinatown was a dying community, with only 88 Chinese still living there.

TAKING ANOTHER LOOK

1. How did the revolution in China in 1911 affect the Chinese in the United States?

2. How did the Exclusion Act affect the opportunities open to Chinese in places like Butte?

3. *CRITICAL THINKING* The Chinese in the United States contributed much money to Sun Yat-sen, the leader of China's 1911 Revolution. Why do you think they did so?

2 A NEW CHINESE AMERICA

How did the Chinese population of the United States change during the late 1800s and early 1900s?

Some of the Chinese who left Butte returned to China. Many had come to the United States as sojourners, never intending to stay. The increasing hostility toward the Chinese in the United States during the late 1800s convinced some of these people that their lives would be better in their homeland. Others, however, chose to stay and committed themselves to building lives in the United States.

Shifts in Population The changes in Butte's Chinese community during the late 1800s and early 1900s were typical of changes in the Chinese American community as a whole. Many of the towns throughout the U.S. West that once had numbers of Chinese residents now had none at all. Chinese Americans shifted from being largely inhabitants of small towns and rural areas to being city dwellers.

Many of the people who once populated the small towns now lived in San Francisco. Others moved east, to Chinatowns in Chicago, Philadelphia, and New York. By 1940, over 70 percent of Chinese Americans would live in cities of at least 100,000.

Most of the Chinese who moved to larger cities did so to have a better chance of making a living. The large Chinatowns of San Francisco and Oak-

Between 1910 and 1940, some 175,000 hopeful Chinese immigrants passed through the immigration station on Angel Island, in San Francisco Bay.

land, California; Portland, Oregon; New York City, and other cities offered employment at a time when many Chinese were being forced out of jobs as a result of prejudice and discrimination.

Yet there were other needs, beyond the need to earn money, that led the Chinese to move to cities. One resident of a Chinatown explained, "Most of us can live a warmer, freer and a more human life among our relatives and friends than among strangers."

Continuing Immigration Many residents of the big-city Chinatowns came not from small towns in the United States, but from small towns in China. Despite the hopes of those who passed them, the Exclusion Act of 1882 and the laws that followed it had not ended Chinese immigration (see graph, page 81). Poor economic conditions in China still encouraged many Chinese to emigrate. Many Chinese also believed that the U.S. exclusion laws were unjust and did not have to be obeyed.

Many Chinese tried to enter the United States by claiming to be U.S. citizens. Under U.S. law, anyone born in the United States is automatically a citizen. Any child of a U.S. citizen is also a citizen. Before 1940, the number of Chinese born in this country was relatively small. But in 1906, a great earthquake and fire almost leveled San Francisco. Large numbers of public records, including birth certificates, went up in flames. One resident of San Francisco's Chinatown explained what that meant:

> [T]he 1906 earthquake came along and destroyed all those immigration things. So that was a big chance for a lot of Chinese. They forged themselves certificates saying that they were born in this country, and when the time came they could go back to China and bring back four or five sons just like that!

Those "sons" were not always the real sons of those who held the forged certificates. Often, they were people who paid money to the holder of a certificate. The certificate holder would then swear that they were his children, thus allowing them to enter the United States. Those who entered the country in this way were called **paper sons.**

ANGEL ISLAND

From 1910 to 1940, most Chinese who hoped to enter the United States passed through the immigration center at Angel Island in San Francisco Bay. There, Chinese arrivals presented their papers for study by immigration inspectors.

The immigrants were subjected to repeated, grueling questioning about their families, their hometowns, and every aspect of their daily lives. Immigration inspectors hoped to find inconsistencies in the stories of the immigrants that would serve as grounds for refusing to admit them to the United States. Questioning could drag on for days and weeks and, in some cases, months and years. During this time, the immigrants were prisoners on the island, forbidden visits by family or friends on the mainland.

Many of the Chinese held on Angel Island carved poems into the wooden walls of the barracks where they lived. Many of the poems have been preserved and translated by the Chinese Cultural Foundation of San Francisco. The following lines are from one of these poems:

> There are tens of thousands of poems composed
>   on these walls.
> They are all cries of complaint and sadness.
> The day I am rid of this prison and attain success,
> I must remember that this prison once existed.

Angel Island is today a California state park. The old barracks has been preserved, keeping alive the memory of the Chinese immigrants and the hardships they endured.

The U.S. government attempted to halt such practices by carefully screening all Chinese immigrants. Between 1910 and 1940, about 10 percent of the Chinese who tried to enter the United States through the immigration center at Angel Island in California (see feature above) were turned back. Some of those rejected were in fact paper sons. Others, however, had a legal right to enter but failed to convince immigration officials.

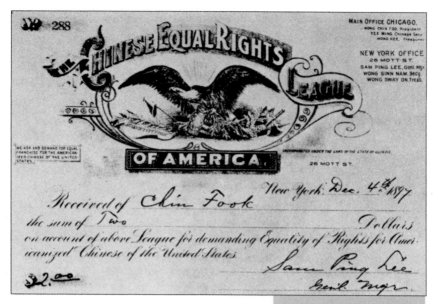

Changing Chinatowns As the Chinatowns of large cities grew, society in those Chinatowns changed. One reason for the change was that larger and larger numbers of Chinese Americans had been born and raised in the United States. In 1900, only 10 percent of the Chinese in the United States had been born here. By 1920, that figure had reached 30 percent. The concerns of these U.S.-born Chinese Americans were chiefly with issues in the United States.

In the past, many of the organizations and associations that developed in Chinatowns had sought to preserve old Chinese ways in the United States. The Chinese Six Companies (see page 28), for example, remained an important organization in Chinatowns across the nation. However, some Chinese believed that the Six Companies was not doing enough to secure their rights.

In 1895, a group of Chinese business leaders who had been born in the United States formed the Native Sons of the Golden State, in San Francisco. The organization fought in court to protect the rights of the Chinese in the United States. The group opposed efforts to segregate Chinese children in public schools. It campaigned against politicians who favored discriminatory laws against the Chinese.

Soon, branches of the organization opened even outside the state. In 1915, the organization changed its name to the Chinese American Citizens' Alliance. The alliance's constitution showed that it was dedicated to reducing the importance of traditional Chinese social organizations. One passage read, "It is imperative [urgent] that no members [of this organization] shall have sectional, clannish, Tong or party prejudices against each other or to use such influences to oppress fellow members."

Signs of Chinese American desire to play a larger part in U.S. society and its institutions became more obvious after the 1911 revolution in China. Many Chinese Americans gave up traditional Chinese clothing and adopted American clothing styles. Chinese Americans began to celebrate such holidays as Independence Day and Thanksgiving. They also started Chinatown branches of such organizations as the Boy Scouts and the YMCA and YWCA.

Yet even as Chinese Americans adopted many of the forms of U.S. society, the attraction of traditional Chinese ways remained strong. Many young Chinese Americans felt torn between two worlds. One man explained:

> I think that both sides are pulling equally—one
> the land of freedom which was my birthplace, my
> home—the other, my parents' home, my race's
> abode and my motherland. In me they both hold
> the same attraction but sometimes America
> seems to get me more over China and I say that if
> any place shall be my home in the old age it *shall*
> be America.

TAKING ANOTHER LOOK

1. How did the Chinese population of the United States change in the years between 1882 and 1920?

2. Why did some Chinese enter the United States as paper sons?

3. *CRITICAL THINKING* Reread the passage from the constitution of the Chinese American Citizens' Alliance above. Why do you think the alliance included this statement in its constitution?

CHAPTER 6: CLOSE UP

1 Responding to Change

- After the Exclusion Act of 1882, many Chinese lost their land, jobs, and businesses.
- Before the Exclusion Act, most Chinese Americans were employed as miners and railroad workers. After it, most worked in laundries and restaurants.
- Chinese Americans in many cities fought labor union boycotts of Chinese-owned businesses.
- A revolution in China in 1911 changed the lives of Chinese in the United States.

2 A New Chinese America

- In the late 1800s and early 1900s, Chinese Americans moved from rural areas and small towns to larger cities in the United States.
- Despite the exclusion laws, people continued to emigrate from China to the United States.
- As the number of Chinese born in the United States grew, they increasingly asserted their identities as American citizens.

WHO, WHAT, WHERE

1. **What** was *hec fu*?
2. **Where** did most Chinese Americans live at the time the Exclusion Act was passed?
3. **What** is a boycott?
4. **Who** was Wilbur Fisk Sanders?
5. **Where** did most Chinese live by 1940?
6. **Where** did a fire provide an opportunity for Chinese to claim U.S. citizenship?
7. **What** was a paper son?
8. **What** was Angel Island?
9. **What** was the Chinese American Citizens' Alliance?

UNDERSTANDING THE CHAPTER

1. Why did Chinese laundries become increasingly mechanized during the late 1800s and early 1900s?

2. How did the 1911 Revolution in China change the lives of the Chinese in the United States?

3. Why did Chinese Americans move from small towns in the United States to larger cities?

4. How did immigrants from China continue to enter the United States after the Exclusion Act?

5. Why did Chinatowns begin to change in the early 1900s?

MAKING CONNECTIONS

1. What was the connection between the changing populations of western towns and the increased difficulty Chinese Americans in these towns had in making a living?

2. What was the connection between the increasing number of Chinese born in the United States and the appearance of new organizations and associations in Chinatowns?

WRITING ABOUT HISTORY

1. Imagine you are a Chinese person who moved from Butte, Montana to San Francisco, California in the early 1900s. Write a letter to your relatives in Butte to convince them to join you.

2. Write a short one-act play about the screening of Chinese immigrants at Angel Island. Characters might be U.S. immigration officials, a Chinese merchant and family, a person with forged documents and his paper sons, and an ailing Chinese immigrant.

3. Angel Island was made into a California state park. Write a funding proposal to the California state government explaining why Angel Island should be preserved.

4. Write an essay describing three ways that prejudice affected Chinese Americans during the late 1800s.

Time Chart

The Time Chart below shows events that were taking place around the world during the years studied in this book.

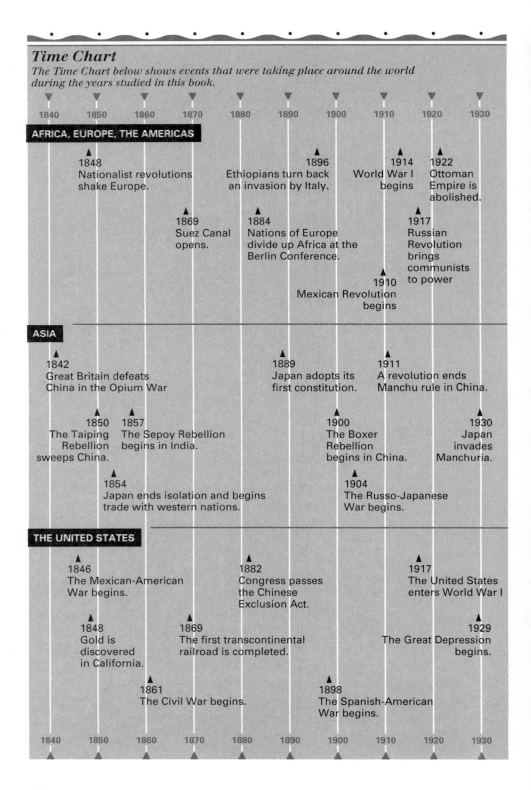

1840 1850 1860 1870 1880 1890 1900 1910 1920 1930

AFRICA, EUROPE, THE AMERICAS

1848
Nationalist revolutions shake Europe.

1896
Ethiopians turn back an invasion by Italy.

1914
World War I begins

1922
Ottoman Empire is abolished.

1869
Suez Canal opens.

1884
Nations of Europe divide up Africa at the Berlin Conference.

1917
Russian Revolution brings communists to power

1910
Mexican Revolution begins

ASIA

1842
Great Britain defeats China in the Opium War

1889
Japan adopts its first constitution.

1911
A revolution ends Manchu rule in China.

1850
The Taiping Rebellion sweeps China.

1857
The Sepoy Rebellion begins in India.

1900
The Boxer Rebellion begins in China.

1930
Japan invades Manchuria.

1854
Japan ends isolation and begins trade with western nations.

1904
The Russo-Japanese War begins.

THE UNITED STATES

1846
The Mexican-American War begins.

1882
Congress passes the Chinese Exclusion Act.

1917
The United States enters World War I

1848
Gold is discovered in California.

1869
The first transcontinental railroad is completed.

1929
The Great Depression begins.

1861
The Civil War begins.

1898
The Spanish-American War begins.

1840 1850 1860 1870 1880 1890 1900 1910 1920 1930

GLOSSARY

The glossary defines important terms used in the book. The page on which a term first appears is given in parentheses at the end of the definition.

artisan craftsworker (17)

assimilate to become absorbed into the main cultural group (70)

barbarians people whose ways of living seem crude or uncivilized (10)

bond sum of money guaranteeing good behavior (67)

boycott to join together in refusing to do business with (80)

Chinese Six Companies several district associations in San Francisco that joined together in the early 1850s and acted as an unofficial government for Chinatown (28)

clan group of families that share a common ancestor (8)

contract workers emigrants who agreed to work for a sponsor for five years in exchange for passage to the United States (13)

cradle rectanglar wooden box mounted on rockers used to sift dirt for gold (23)

depression period in which there is severe economic decline (66)

dialect form of language spoken in a particular region (7)

discriminate to treat people unfairly, especially people of minority groups (63)

emigrate to leave one's home country for another place (4)

fong Chinese family association (27)

hsiang **(sheeang)** hometown or village (4)

huiguan **(hwee-gwan)** Chinese district association (28)

innovator person who introduces new methods, devices, or ideas (46)

Isthmus of Panama narrow strip of land where North and South America meet (33)

junk flat bottomed Chinese sailing ship (9)

literate able to read and write

pan to sift dirt from a riverbed with a pan to find gold (23)

paper son person who was brought to the United States by a Chinese who held U.S. citizenship and falsely claimed that person was his child (85)

regional group group of people who share common history, language, customs, and traditions (7)

sojourner someone who comes for a visit and then returns home (27)

steerage part of a ship, often in the cargo hold, where the poorest passengers traveled (20)

Taiping Rebellion unsuccessful rebellion against the Manchu dynasty, 1850–1864 (11)

tenant farmer person who farms land owned by someone else and gives the landlord a share of the crop in exchange for the use of the land and tools (48)

terrace great step carved on a hillside to add more land for crops (6)

tong Chinese secret society; sometimes became involved in illegal practices (29)

trestle bridge made of vertical or slanting beams (39)

yuen companies formed by Chinese tenant farmers whose members were collectively responsible for leasing and running a farm (48)

INDEX

SOURCES

Sources for quotations are given by page number (in parentheses) and in the order in which the quotations appear on each page. **CHAPTER 1** **(4)** Poem, quoted in Lynn Pan, *Sons of the Yellow Emperor* (New York: Little, Brown, 1990), p. 21. **CHAPTER 2** **(16)** Pyau Ling, from *Annals of the Academy of Political and Social Sciences,* quoted in Stan Steiner, *Fusang: The Chinese Who Built America* (New York: Harper & Row, 1979), p. 107. **(18)** Minister and miner, quoted in Steiner, p. 109. **(19)** Lai Chun-Chuen, quoted in Ronald Takaki, *Strangers From a Different Shore* (Boston: Little, Brown, 1989), p. 37. "Friends in China," speech quoted in Takaki, p. 81. **(20)** "Some have borrowed," quoted in Takaki, p. 35. Huie Kin, Reminiscences (Peiping, 1932), p. 55. **(21)** Huie Kin, p. 56. **(26)** San Francisco newspaper, quoted in Linda Perrin, *Coming to America* (New York: Delacorte, 1980), p. 16. **(29)** Letter to governor, *Daily Alta,* 1852, quoted in Takaki, p. 112. **CHAPTER 3** **(34)** Reporter, quoted in Dee Brown, *Hear That Lonesome Whistle Blow* (New York: Holt, 1977), p. 94. **(38)** Chief engineer, quoted in Corinne K. Hoexter, *From Canton to California: The Epic of Chinese Immigration* (New York: Four Winds Press, 1976), pp. 86-87. **(42)** Crocker, quoted in Hoexter, p. 87. **CHAPTER 4** **(46)** "They started everything," quoted in Victor G. Nee and Brett De Bary, *Longtime Californ': A Documentary Study of an American Chinatown* (New York: Pantheon, 1972). p. 77. **(48-49)** "Potato king," based on information in Ruthanne Lum McCunn, *Chinese American Portraits* (San Francisco: Chronicle Books, 1988). **(50-51)** Poem, from Marion K. Hom, *Songs of Gold Mountains: Cantonese Rhythms from San Francisco Chinatown* (Berkeley, CA: University of California, 1987), p. 96. **(51)** Lee Chew, quoted in Takaki, p. 92-93. **(53)** Novel, quoted in Milton Meltzer, *The Chinese Americans* (New York: Thomas Y. Crowell, 1980) pp. 91-92. **(53-54)** Wong Sing, based on information in McCunn. **(56-57)** Woman immigrant in 1869, quoted in Takaki, p. 124. **(57)** Sebastapol settlement, quoted in Nee and De Bary. **(57-59)** Yun Oi and Mary Bong, based on information in McCunn. **CHAPTER 5** **(64)** Merchant, quoted in Takaki, p. 114. **(64-65)** Court decision, *People v. Hall,* 4 *Cal.* 309 (1854). **(65)** Civil Rights Act, quoted in Takaki, p. 114. **(65-66)** Mark Twain, *Roughing It* (Berkeley, CA: University of California, 1972) p. 116. **(66)** Song, in *The Blue and Grey Songster* (San Francisco: S.S. Green, 1877). **(67)** "Drive [the Chinese] to other states," quoted in Roger Daniels, *Asian America: Chinese and Japanese in the United States Since 1850* (Seattle: University of Washington, 1988), p. 39. **(69)** Henry George editorial, New York *Tribune,* May 1, 1869. **(70)** U.S. workers, quoted in U.S. Congress, *Misc. Document 81,* 42d Cong. 3d sess, 1873. **(70)** Charles Sumner, in *The Works of Charles Sumner* (Boston: Lee and Shepard, 1870-1883), vol. 13, p. 483. **(71)** Majority report, in U.S. Congress, Senate, *Report of the Joint Special Committee to Investigate Chinese Immigration, Report 689,* 44th Cong., 2d sess., 1877, pp. iii-viii. **(73)** Rancher, quoted in David H. Stratton, "The Snake River Massacre of Chinese Miners, 1887," in Duane A. Smith, ed., *A Taste of the West,* p.125. **(74)** Chinese ambassador, quoted in "Law and the Chinese in Frontier Montana," *Montana* 30, no.3 (1980), p. 31. **(75)** Chinese American writer, quoted in Meltzer, p. 135. **CHAPTER 6** **(78)** Poem, quoted in Steiner, p. 78. **(81)** Chinese woman in Butte, quoted in Daniels, p. 81. **(82)** Butte laundryman, quoted in Daniels, p. 79. **(84)** Chinatown resident, quoted in Ching-Chao Wu, "Chinatowns: A Study in Symbiosis and Assimilation" (dissertation: University of Chicago, 1928), p. 158. "The 1906 earthquake," in Nee and De Bary, p. 63. **(85)** Poem, quoted in Mark Him Lai, Genny Lim, and Judy Yung, *Island: Poetry and History of Chinese Immigrants on Angel Island, 1910-1940* (San Francisco: San Francisco Study Center, 1981), p.66. **(87)** Young Chinese American, quoted in Takaki, p. 260.